Nostradamus

and the

Planets of Apocalypse

New Evidence for the
Global Disasters Coming
in 2040 and 2046 AD

by

Jason M. Breshears

THE BOOK TREE
San Diego, California

ISBN 978-1-58509-140-9

Cover images (excluding Nostradamus portrait)
copyright by sdecoret

Portrait of Michel de Nostredame (Nostradamus) painted by his son, César de Nostredame (1553-1630?) about 1614 A.D., now possessed by the Bibliothèque Méjanes in Aix-en-Provence, France.

Cover layout by
Atulya Berube

Published by
The Book Tree
P O Box 16476
San Diego, CA 92176
www.thebooktree.com

We provide fascinating and educational products to help awaken the public to new ideas and information that would not be available otherwise.
Call 1 (800) 700-8733 for our FREE BOOK TREE CATALOG.

*There will come a time when none of the secrets of
nature will be out of the reach of the human mind.*

—Matthias Quadt, 1599 AD

CONTENTS

Preface

2040 AD. . .

There are people preparing, even now, for the total collapse of human civilization that will occur in May, 2040 AD. As this is being written we have 28 years remaining, a period relatively short when considering that only 28 years ago it was 1984.

The world as we know it, the trans-cultural, global civilization that we have built, the technological comforts, the freedoms, environmental and personal protections, all these will come to a sudden and violent end in 2040. In the month of May a vast, dark celestial object will pass directly between the earth and sun, transiting closer than Venus and during the occult of the solar orb the sky will darken, day will be turned into night, our planet bathed in an immense debris field from space with gigantic rocks, ice and billions of tons of dirt and dust.

Our world has suffered this several times before throughout its long past and these prior visitations of planet Phoenix have been well-documented in this author's prior work entitled *When the Sun Darkens,* published in 2009. It will return on its easily detectable orbit in May of 2040, a fact known to our predecessors, known to scientists who are dissuaded from publicizing their findings and as will be shown in this book, a fact well known to the French prophet Nostradamus.

After May of 2040 there will be no more high school graduations, summer vacations, no more Super Bowls, presidential elections, social networking sites or even an Internet. The thousands of satellites orbiting our planet will be destroyed and those still functioning will have nothing on the surface of the world to relay data to. The Olympics will be a thing of the past, the 4th of July will not be a time of celebration, at Thanksgiving families will not sit at tables eating turkey and feasts. . . survivors will be starving in their daily search for something to eat amidst the rubble and ash. At Christmas there will be no good will toward men, but men and women will be hunted as cannibalism plagues the wasted cities of the nations.

No more fast food, restaurants, fields filled with produce and grains, no hospitals, no television, no constitutional rights nor police to enforce them. Gone will be the days of governmental organization of society, for warlords will rule their urban kingdoms with gangs of armed men. Entire peaceful communities that survive the cataclysm will be invaded as marauders seeking their supplies and resources will slay and enslave those unable to come together and defend what they have left.

Women, young girls and boys will be brutalized, raped, tortured and eaten, the strong preying on the weak for sexual satisfaction and sustenance. A woman will become more precious than fine gold. They will be enslaved, used in barter for gear, food and weapons. Captured males will be used to entertain the people in abandoned superdomes and arenas in horrific blood sports mirroring the coliseum of Roman times. As anarchy prevails, a New Stone Age emerges with strange religions and cults defying the Lord of Heaven, as men become worshipped and human sacrifices resurrect from the elder way of pagan times. A new civilization of barbarity will arise in 2040 after a quarter of the world's population dies. Dictators form new governments and republicanism and democracy disappear as relics of antiquity. In those days the people still seeking God are an extreme minority.

This new culture of chaos will not endure long. Another catastrophe awaits and will transpire six years later in 2046 AD. Another long-period orbiting gigantic planet known well to the ancients will return and almost collide into Earth. This is NIBIRU, the subject of this author's book called *Anunnaki Homeworld*, which fully details its orbital chronology and effect in visitations long ago. These two planets, seen and known to modern astronomers who have been effectively silenced by academic peers, international organizations that fund scientific research and by governmental operatives, will reappear in 2040 and 2046 from far north of the ecliptic [Phoenix] and from far below it [NIBIRU] to usher in the dreaded Apocalypse.

Two global destructions await us, back-to-back, and *both* were seen by the prophet Nostradamus. Both are fully detailed in the prophecies of the ancients spread across the world. Both were seen and recorded by the prophetess Ursula Southeil. . . and Nostradamus has told us very clearly to beware the month of *May* in 2040 AD.

With thousands of books about the French prophet it is truly astounding that no one has until now understood how it was possible for him to so accurately see the future, to determine his *method* of seeing the future. It will be shown herein that the prophecies of Nostradamus were *dated* and that this discovery of a Date-Index was recently published by Mario Reading.

What is so astonishing is that Nostradamus predicted these global destructions for the years 2040 and 2046 AD, which perfectly align with orbital periodicities of two gigantic planets expounded upon in *When the Sun Darkens* and *Anunnaki Homeworld*. This is beyond coincidence. Nostradamus was not merely a prophet—he *chronicled* the future.

How any of us can do the same is revealed in this book.

I

Introduction to Calendrical Isometrics

The horror comes in reality from the mathematical aspect of the event. . . no code of
ethics are justifiable a priori in the face of the
cruel mathematics that command our condition.   —*Albert Camus* (1)

In 1973 the World Trade Center towers were completed in New York City. At that time, standing 110 stories each, they were the tallest buildings in the world. On February 21 of the same year an Israeli jet shot down a Libyan passenger jet killing 103 people. These two events would appear to be unconnected, occurring in opposite hemispheres, to be separated in both time and space.

The destruction of the World Trade Center towers in 2001, popularly remembered as 911, is a day not easily erased from the mind of Americans. It is the one day in our collective pasts that each and every one of us today knows exactly what we were doing on that dark day. In the complex geometrical matrix of our lives we know today precisely the *time* and *location* of our experiences as 911 occurred.

But was this a predictable event? Is there a correlation between the World Trade Center destruction and the destruction of a Libyan passenger jet 28 years earlier? Is there a definite method by which anyone could predict a future event? Could it be possible that the future of anything is hewn from its history?

The answer to all of these questions is yes.

What you are going to read in this book will change your life. Like stopping to read a very important monument along the side of the road, this book will change your path; for once the human mind is stretched by a new idea it can never go back to its original dimensions.(2) In order to fully comprehend how truly easy it is for one to see the future we must understand the findings of some of the greatest minds that ever lived.

Albert Einstein believed that time itself was a geometrical concept.(3) This world-famous physicist said, "The future . . . is every whit as necessary and *determined as the past*,"(4) and that "People like us, who believe in physics, know that the distinctions between the past, present and future is only a stubbornly persistent illusion."(5) Einstein's opinion was not dissimilar from other great scientific minds. The Russian physicist P.D. Ouspensky in the early 20th century in his epic work *Tertium Organum* wrote, "Future events are wholly contained in preceding ones, and if we could know the force and direction of all events which have happened up to the present moment, i.e. if we knew all the past, by this we could know *all the future*."(6) He too believed that time was a geometrical construction embedded within the human psyche. He further wrote, "The past and future are existing simultaneously on the lines perpendicular to our plane, and the *past is identical* with the future because phenomena come from both sides and go in both *directions*."(7)

If this is true then this concept must be demonstrated. If demonstration can be replicated many times then a fundamental aspect of our existence has been discovered. If the phenomenon of an event is moving in two directions in time and space at the same time then we can perceive our space-time structure as acting similar to the ripples on the surface of a pool of water. An event happening right now in the present would correspond to the epicenter of a concentric pattern of wave-rings rippling up the surface of the pool after a drop of water fell upon the smooth surface. The ripples traveling to the left would symbolize *past events* while those moving toward the right were *future occurrences*. No matter how far the ripples travel they will always be equidistant from the epicenter of the ring formation. Each wave-ring is the same distance from the center as the corresponding wave-ring on the other side of the pool.

If this thesis is to be demonstrated and explained, then we need to apply fixed terms to the particulars of this phenomenon. For our purposes here the drop [event] that creates the space-time structure [wave-rings] that issue out in both directions [past and future] is the center of the entire pattern. Thus, this is the *Isometric Epicenter*. The word isometric denotes something that goes in two directions at the same time, and in this case, we are referring to timelines [wave-rings]. The epicenter is *any event* in history that one would want to know the future of.

The future of an event is represented by the wave-rings that travel to the right. But as these are merely the geometrical reflections of the same events that traveled to the left [past], then to understand the future events we must compare them with those that are equidistant from the *Isometric Epicenter*. For example, the third wave-ring to the right [future] is a reflection of the third wave-ring to the left [past], the fourth or seventeen and so on. This is an *Isometric Projection*, the comparative analysis of an observer [historian or prophet] of two events, one in the past and one in the future, both connected to a central event geometrically. This is *calendrical isometrics*.

We take for our isometric epicenter the year 1973. This was the beginning [foundation] of the timelines involving the city of New York, passenger jets destroyed, and the World Trade Center towers. As we have stated, these buildings in New York were the tallest towers in the world. The Israelis shot down a Libyan passenger jet killing 103 people. In retrospect we know that passenger jets were used to destroy the World Trade Center towers in 2001 and that this was *28 years* after the World Trade Center was completed. We may never know the truth as to why the Israelis shot down the Libyan jet but we do know that Libya is a thriving terrorist base of operations and sanctuary. Now, 2001 is 28 wave-rings from 1973, it being the future [2001] that unfolded after 1973. Studying its geometrical reflection of 28 wave-rings [years] prior to 1973 we come to the year 1945 and to a most remarkable and little-remembered event in American history that was *never* mentioned by the media during the 911 episode. In 1945 a U.S. B-25 Bomber piloted by Lt. Colonel William Smith crashed right through the 78-79th floors of the *tallest building in the world*, the Empire State Building, in *New York City*. The pilot was flying through low fog clouds and lost his bearings. The space-time reflection is hauntingly precise. It was United Airlines Flight 175 that slammed into the South Tower's 79th and 80th floors, a wing even striking the 78th floor according to David Icke in *Alice in Wonderland and the World Trade Center Disaster*.

This is a modern-day example of calendrical isometrics. Had an observer been aware of this little-remembered event in 1945 when considering the completion of the World Trade Center towers in 1973 as the tallest buildings on earth in that year (superseded in 1974 by other towers) then this person could have conducted an Isometric Projection that would have revealed the year 2001 as a terrible day in New York among its skyscrapers. The end of any thing is always connected to its beginning. Over eighteen centuries ago this was recognized by Origen in *De Principiis* when he wrote, "For the end is always like the beginning."(8)

Every event of every second in space and time is geometrically connected isometrically to both past and future times and events. By analogy, our space-time structure is like this same pool of water, but instead of a single drop disturbing the smooth surface into a pattern of ever-growing rings, every fraction of our own existence is permeated with wave-ripples from countless events from countless times that create interference patterns that slightly alter the future wave-rings [events] so that they never quite mirror exactly their past counterparts [wave-rings].

This is why there are slight deviations and that no future event can totally replicate a similar event in the past. But the phenomenon is real. It is demonstrable and the ancients understood the concept. To continue with our analogy, the fabric of reality is this pool of water, as it would appear as thousands of raindrops slammed into its already rippling surface, forming patterns within patterns. The ripples [events] do not hinder one another as they transect. They flow through one another. The space-time interface of multiple timelines all operating simultaneously is the cause for the effect we erroneously refer to as *coincidence*.

Our predecessors believed that the knowledge of the future was accessible by the study of the past. A golden inscription discovered in the famous tomb of King Tutankhamen of Egypt reads, "I have seen the past; I know the future. (9) King Esarhaddon of Assyria in the 7th century BC left behind an inscribed tablet saying, "The future shall be like the past."(10) King Jedidiyah, better known to history as Solomon who ruled the united kingdom of Israel and Judah wrote: "That which hath been is now; and that which is to be hath already been; and God requireth that *which is past*."

In more recent antiquity we find this belief unchanged. In the apocryphal Gospel of Thomas we find Jesus saying, "Have you then deciphered the beginning, that you ask about the end? For where the beginning is, there shall be an end . . . blessed is the man who reaches the beginning, he will *know the end*." About three centuries later the Jewish Rabbi Hillel III wrote, "After having viewed our present condition, it may be for us to look back and review our former history, and get a knowledge of the state of the world in former times." From that same period the Christian writer Augustine of Hippo in *City of God* wrote, "The things which then were hidden are now sufficiently revealed by the actual events *which have followed*."(11) Because the phenomenon of the passage of events through the space-time structure has the quality of being isometric, traveling both into the past and future simultaneously, scholars five centuries ago like Firmicus Maternus could declare that "The beginning of anything was to be found out by the unfolding of *historical events*."(12)

More contemporary philosophers and historians have not deviated from this tenet. In his *Discourses* Niccolo Machievelli made two statements that capture our attention: "If one examines with diligence the past, it is easy to foresee the future." Then he goes on to remark: "He who would foresee what has to be, should reflect on what has been, for everything that happens in the world at any time has a genuine resemblance to what happened in ancient times."(13) Machievelli had conducted extensive researches on the history of Europe to produce his more famous works known as *The Prince* and *The Art of War*. There are few men alive that can boast of having read and researched more on our world's ancient beliefs and histories than Gerald Massey, author of the huge volumes entitled *Ancient Egypt: Light of the World* and *The Natural Genesis*. These monstrous volumes are packed with historical, anthropological and mythological data. Massey's *Lectures* from the 1880s were published and in them he made these statements: "The past is a region to explore . . . it is impossible to understand the present without the profoundest knowledge of the past." And, "Our past deeds must and *will* make our future fate."(14)

A contemporary of Massey was the occultist Franz Hartmann, who, in 1888 published a work on magic. Hartmann perceived that the entire universe is made up of matter that vibrates at different frequencies, which gives various materials the densities they have. This is now a known fact about all physical objects concerning this illusory world that still mystifies the quantum physicists. The number of vibrations at a given interval is what identifies something from something else. What interests us here is that Hartmann wrote: "If everything has a certain number of vibrations, and if these vibrations increase or diminish at a certain ratio and in regular periods, a *knowledge of these numbers* will enable us to *predict a future event*."(15) Oswald Spengler in his famous *The Decline of the West* commented that ". . .the most valuable thing in the classical mathematic is its proposition that *number* is the essence of all things *perceptible to the senses*.(16)

Calendrical isometrics is the science of the future. Instead of counting vibrations, the historian or prophet counts *years* as his numbers, which are represented by the wave-rings upon the surface of the pool. A very relevant statement was uttered in 1902 AD by Judge Thomas Troward when he said, "The more deeply we investigate the world we live in, the more clear it must become to us that all our science is the translation into words or *numerical symbols* of that order which already exists."(17) Numbers serve as the alphabet in this method of analyzing history and the future, but it is the backward and forward isometric timelines that construct *sentences* out of these numerical letters we employ. And multiple isometric projections all linked to the *same year* form for us entire paragraphs, pages and even a whole book of knowledge about a future event.

There are so many isometric timelines ending on 2040 AD and others ending on 2046 AD that the reader will be astounded when finishing this book. Never again will you see the past or the future in the same light and many readers will be offended that they were raised in institutions of learning that actually served to impede their understanding of the past so they could not accurately see beyond the now. The famous critical thinker Rene Descartes wrote, "It were far better to never think of investigating truth at all, than to do so without a method."(18) Our method is to study what occurred during certain years. When they reveal isometric patterns we are offered a window into the past to preceding events that molded the conditions in time and space for the other events that followed. Through the study of calendrical isometrics we see more clearly who we are and where we came from . . . two requirements necessary when considering *where* we are going.

Our present blindness is partly because we have been duped by historians and chronologists over and over again into accepting that any particular calendar is in itself important, that the artificial phenomenon of mechanical time governs our existence. Nothing could be further from the truth. The historian Lewis Mumford summed it up perfectly in his monumental work entitled *Technics and Civilization* when he wrote, "Time is measured not by the calendar but by the events that occupy it."(19)

History is the surface of our pool of water. Though it is a surface, a plane, it has depth and the spatial dimensions to accompany an infinitude of timelines. Innumerous drops of water [events] rain onto the pool creating countless patterns [timelines], some even intersecting one another but still remain a part of their own inertia as they flow through myriads of other times and places. Oswald Spengler contributes to this analogy, writing: "Over the expanse of the water pass the endless uniform ripples of the generations. Here and there bright shafts of light broaden out, everywhere dancing flashes confuse and disturb the clear mirror, changing. Sparkling, vanishing. These are what we call the clans, tribes, peoples, races which unify a series of generations within this or that limited area of the historical surface . . . but over this surface, too, the great cultures accomplish their majestic wave-cycles. They appear suddenly, swell in splendid lines, flatten again and vanish, and the face of the waters is once more a sleeping waste."(20) Many, many timelines can all be connected to the same year [wave-ring] as will now be shown.

Although 1973 AD was the epicentral year in our study of the World Trade Center this does not in any way restrict 1973 from being a part of other isometric projections. Many events occurred in 1973 and for every single individual event there are isometric projections because this phenomenon is the motive force that builds our everyday reality. At 20 miles per second our planet flows through space, orbiting the sun, while we flow through an incomprehensibly vast space-time structure virtually saturated with unseen events in motion. Current events are the space-time reflections of future phenomena not yet passed through.

In the year 1054 AD the entire world witnessed a stunning heavenly sight when a star exploded in the Crab Nebula and the nova brightened the night skies. In this same year Pope Leo IX of the Roman Papacy excommunicated the Patriarch of Constantinople, which resulted in a great rift between the Eastern Orthodox Church and the Church of Rome which ruled from the Vatican. This division embroiled all the nations of Europe, initiating feuds and wars. Christianity emerged directly out of the roots of Judaism and the older Israelite scriptures. The two elements of 1054 that grab our attention are *religious division* and *war*. With 1054 now our epicentral date we now examine 1973 a little more closely. The most widely televised and internationally recognized events transpiring in 1973 was the Islamic invasion of Israel in the amazing Yom Kippur War, again, involving the elements of religion and war involving Jews instead of Christians. Muslims were also involved in the 2001 destruction of the World Trade Center towers.

The 1973 Yom Kippur War saw Israel up against incredible odds and vastly outnumbered and surrounded, yet, to the world's astonishment, the Israeli's defended themselves and beat back their enemies. This occurred *919 years* after the 1054 epicentral year, and counting *919 years* before the epicentral year of 1054 AD we arrive at the tragic date of 135 AD when Judea was surrounded by the *Romans*, terribly outmatched and outnumbered, and Jerusalem was sieged. This was the Bar Kochba Rebellion against Rome, meaning *Son of a Star*. The Jews were crushed, their city taken apart and destroyed and the survivors were crucified and sold into the slave markets of the Mediterranean. Both the beginning and the end of the Isometric Projection found the Jews badly outnumbered and at war with foreign peoples, the circumstances the same with only the outcomes differing. There are so many easily shown isometric projections throughout history that this author is preparing an entire book full of them.

That every future is an echo of its past is demonstrated by this peculiar forward and backward trait embedded within the geometrical framework of history. Could it be possible that some men are influenced by a future that exists in space but has not yet transpired in time? Every second we spend in the present we are held together by an infinite amount of *pasts* as well as *futures* – we as humans are virtually trapped at the intersect point between two infinities. If the future did not yet exist somewhere then *we could not exist either*. The space-time sequence of events is moored to something, be it a property of our collective psyche or an Eternal Mind (if there is a difference), somewhere, the future exists in space though unrealized in time. This was the belief one thousand five hundred years ago of Augustine of Hippo, who wrote:

> Where did those who sang prophecies see
> these events if they do not yet exist? To see
> what has no existence is impossible. And
> those who narrate past history would surely
> not be telling a true story if they did not dis-
> cern events by their soul's insight. If the past
> were nonexistent, it could not be discerned at
> all. Therefore, both future and past exist.(21)

And because it exists, interwoven into the matrix of the present and past, it is accessible. Our minds are open to every impression that touches us as we flow through our environments. We traverse our lives through a medium of innumerable contacts, immersed in an uncountable multitude of places that remain nonlocal because physically we can only experience one *time* at a time. For this reason we are sometimes overcome with the sensation that we already know something that we also know we had never learned; that we had seen or experienced something before though we have no memory of it, or the feeling that we are being watched takes over us; that we have performed certain acts exactly in the same way we had done them in the unremembered past. The sensations of déjà vu, occurrences of retrocognition, synchronicity and coincidence are reminders that the world around us that we perceive through the agency of our limited senses is far greater in depth than we are able to grasp.

That prophets have foretold many recorded events long prior to their unfolding in the human drama is well attested in the literature of nations around the world, spanning back centuries and even millennia. What has not been known is how they do it. We are given the answer that these men and women were touched by the Divine, and this may be so. We are created beings, and incidentally, encoded within our own biological programs are precise geometrical informations. There appears to be a direct connection between our external space-time structured existence in material reality and our internal *genetic* geometrical DNA structure. The *forward and backward* property expounded upon in this work concerning historical timelines is scientifically referred to as a *palindrome*. This is a sequence of numbers that count both forward and backward from an epicentral point. Intriguingly, it has been discovered that much of our DNA is structured in the form of palindromes, as yet "undeciphered sentences," that read both forward and backward, mystifying the geneticists. In fact, perhaps as much as 95% of our DNA remains undeciphered according to Sol Luckman in *Conscious Healing.* (22) If this is the foundation of our body in the microscopic realm in which our psyche inhabits, then naturally this is also a property of the universe we are suspended within. The macrocosm merely reflects the microcosm. Isometric Projections are real and measurable in the outer world of experiences because they reflect the inner world of man.

Isometric Projections demonstrate that:

(1)   a system of historical analysis is available by which Nostradamus could have based his prophecies;

(2)   a review of isometric projections *proves* the dates of Nostradamus.

The prophecies of Nostradamus are so detail-specific concerning the return of planet Phoenix that the reader must be familiar somewhat about Phoenix and what happened to the earth in former times when it passed closely by. The next chapter reviews this history, which is more fully detailed in *When the Sun Darkens*; however, because this author has found so much more *new* evidence in support of the Phoenix Chronology, he has avoided reciting those already well documented points in his prior book. This chapter unveils all the new Phoenix-related discoveries and data, information that no doubt Nostradamus also had access to.

Interestingly, Nostradamus wrote that his own method of divining the future was by looking into a *pool of water*. Was this a clever hint?

II

Planet Phoenix: Keeper of the Calendar

"All certainty which does not consist in
mathematical demonstration is nothing
more than the highest probability; there is
no other historical certainty." —*Voltaire* (1)

The entire orbital chronology of planet Phoenix as it visited the inner solar
system every 138 years is found in *When the Sun Darkens*. This chapter will
only concentrate on those new findings confirming the existence and orbit of
Phoenix. In the back of this book is a complete, abbreviated chronological
timeline of the orbits of Phoenix and NIBIRU.

The 4309 BC destruction of the Pre-Adamic World was caused by a
close Phoenix transit that resulted in the total ruination of the world and is
the subject matter of the ancient Babylonian *Enuma Elish* tablets copied from
older Sumerian texts that convey that the Earth was originally *from the Deep*.
This is a reference to the Abyss, a region of southern space far south of the
ecliptic below the sun we orbit.(2) This early cosmological text relates an
ancient solar system cataclysm involving the destruction of planets and their
rearrangement.

This catastrophe is reflected in the Egyptian Gnostic text called the
Trimorphic Protennoia, which conveys that the gods [planets] were made
fearful because the *body of ascent* [planet emerging from Abyss] was destroyed
by a thunder in the Deep [Abyss] caused by a great fire [nova] that overturned
their *thrones* [planets were called thrones by the ancients]. These Archons
[Lords of Time: i.e. planetary motion] said, "Our entire habitation has been
shaken, and the entire circuit of our *path of ascent* [orbit] has been met with
destruction, and the path [orbit] upon which we go."(3) This text depicts an
altered planetary orbit. The Gnostics had the advantage of using the famous

Library of Alexandria, which was packed with volumes of translations from texts all around the known world.

Another Gnostic text discovered among the Nag Hammadi artifacts in 1945 is entitled *On the Origin of the World*. This text actually *names* Phoenix and reads that it was a witness against the powers of darkness, a witness against the angels. Phoenix was appointed to remain until the Consummation [an end by destruction]. Phoenix is a witness in the heavens just as are the sun and moon, which associates it to a *celestial body*. Phoenix appears as a sign to the world of what will occur in the end when the *sun will darken* and the moon cease shining, the oceans becoming agitated and the world erupts in chaos.(4)

Planet Phoenix brings with it an extensive strewn field of hundreds of thousands of miles of dust, dirt, small rocks and ice to gigantic asteroids and glacial masses that break free of its surface when approaching the inner solar system, much of it blanketing Earth. During direct transits it is this enveloping of debris that darkens the sun. In the mystical traditions published in *The Holy Tablets* which cite thousands of references to Sumerian, Akkadian and Babylonian texts, we learn that the world was inhabited before Adam and Eve but destroyed when a *dust cloud hid the sun* and meteorites fell upon the Earth. This ruination is why the beginning of Genesis reads, "and there was darkness over the face of the deep."(5) This same dust cloud that destroyed Earth in 4309 BC will return many times throughout the world's history and was even mentioned by Nostradamus.

The Great Flood was caused by a comet collision seven days after Phoenix transited, darkening the sun. These records, legends and evidences are provided in *When the Sun Darkens* and *Anunnaki Homeworld*. The Deluge was a near total destruction of the planet. It occurred in the 1656th year of the Old World's calendar and the biblical chronologist Stephen Jones dates this event at 2239 BC, precisely in accord with the orbits of Phoenix. The Jews claim that the Flood happened in the 1656th year and Augustine wrote this as well.(6) Frank Joseph in *Survivors of Atlantis* provides us with two new pieces of evidence. He claims that an analysis of ancient Chinese traditions using royal chronologies places the Emperor Shun in 2240 BC (one year variance) witnessing a large meteor falling from the sky to strike the earth, followed by a flooding.(7) Further, he claims that in 1998 W. Bruce Masse, an environmental archeologist with the U.S. Air Force revealed that the ancient world was plagued by a series of catastrophic cosmic impacts, with one colliding into earth approximately 2240 BC.(8) Again, this approximate is only *one* year off. French scientists studying the strata below the Middle East found layers of calcite indicating a cosmic impact or several impacts around 2200 BC, according to Colin Wilson in his *Atlantis and the Kingdom of the Neanderthals* on page 89. For an approximate, this too is rather close.

Exactly 552 years after the Great Flood the planet Phoenix darkened the sun and caused earthquakes that destroyed megalithic cities and monuments all around the world. This sun-darkening episode interrupted a battle between the sons of Jacob and the Amorite-led Canaanite armies as detailed in the *Book of Jasher*. Entire civilizations vanished and even today their gigantic monuments remain as silent reminders that the level of culture and engineering in antiquity far surpasses what is currently believed by academia.

After *When the Sun Darkens* was published in 2009 this author read a large book by W. J. Perry on the Archaic Civilization entitled *Children of the Sun,* first published in 1923. He provides an overwhelming wealth of knowledge that the ruling families and dynasties around the world during the Old Bronze Age referred to themselves as Children of the Sun. But then something happened. The entire Archaic Civilization, which was widespread, erupted into chaos and violence as states began warring with one another ". . .about 1688 BC." This is only 1 year off from this author's previously researched date (see *When the Sun Darkens*) of 1687 BC for a major Phoenix transit. For Perry, this is amazingly accurate for a man writing of events 36 centuries later. He states that after this date the regents stopped referring to themselves as Children of the Sun, but he admits he does not know why. As the readers of this author's prior works would know, the ancients lost faith in the sun because *it had failed them*. What was supposed to be impossible – the sun's loss of power – happened through the mysterious darkening caused by the transit of Phoenix. Interestingly, and entirely coincidental, Perry's book, counting the title page, is exactly 552 pages in length, 552 years being a Phoenix Cycle. A Phoenix Cycle was four orbits of Phoenix, each being 138 years. Equating the blackening of the solar orb with the quakes that leveled their stone cities, the leaders of the Archaic Civilization no longer used the sun as a dynastic reference.

Another important reference to 1687 BC Phoenix transit was recently found by the author in the writings of Augustine, preserving the chronological histories of the Roman historian Marcus Varro. Argos was a thriving pre-Greek kingdom in the Peloponnesus ruled by king Phoroneus. At this time the Flood of Ogyges occurred, a disaster afflicting much of the coastal lands around the Mediterranean and Aegean seas. Augustine, citing Varro's *Of the Race of the Roman People* wrote, "There occurred a remarkable celestial portent, for Castor records that, in the brilliant star Venus, called Vesperugo by Plautus and the lovely Hesperus by Homer, there occurred a strange prodigy, that it changed its color, size, form, course, which never happen before nor since. Adrastus of Cyzicus, and Dion of Naples, famous mathematicians, said that this occurred in the reign of Ogyges."(9) That the ancients witnessed a large planetary body approach the earth cannot be contested but the assessment that this was the planet Venus is easily challenged. Venus still maintains the same orbit, unchanged for millennia and never could it come close enough to earth for us to notice an increase in size and then for it to return to its former orbital belt. However, the mistake was an easy one to make. Planet Phoenix on its north-to-south passage through the inner system intersects the plane of the ecliptic directly between the orbits of Venus and Earth, which is why it occasionally darkens the sun, but *only* in May. Every year in our planet's trip around the sun, which is 93 million miles away, we pass through the exact same space in May. Like a celestial clock, this is without fail. Every 138 years Phoenix passes very close to this region but if Earth is somewhere else on its orbit around the sun we miss it entirely. The ancients noticed that the intruder came from the region of space occupied by Venus, which was closer to the sun, making the obvious assumption that it was Venus, though it was not. Amazingly, Frank Joseph in *Survivors of Atlantis* makes the astute observation that the Hittites at this time also made the same mistake. In this stunning research Joseph provides a wealth of data obtained from scientists around the world showing that a massive global disaster occurred approximately 1629-1628 BC (58-59 years off). He cites the discovery that in the 9th year of king Amaziduga of the Hittites the king recorded the appearance of a great celestial body called NINSIANNA. Joseph notes that other researchers automatically associate it with the planet Venus!(10) This NINSIANNA is none other than Phoenix.

In the ancient Egyptian city of On [Annu/Heliopolis] was housed the Mansion of the Phoenix, where the benben was placed – an old fragment of a meteorite. The Egyptians believed that the disappearances and appearances of the Divine Bennu Bird [Phoenix] were ". . .linked to violent cosmic cycles and to the destruction and rebirth of world ages."(11) An Egyptian papyrus written in Greek but dated as a copy from an older text from the time of Amenhotep, reads, ". . .for in the Typhon time the sun is veiled."(12) This dates to 1576-1555 BC. That Typhon is etymologically akin to Phoenix is clearly seen: Ty[phon] and [Phoen]ix. The oldest images of the Phoenix were of the date palm, a slender tree in Egypt sacred to the *reckoning of times*. In fact, date palms were called phoenix palms. This most arcane symbolism regarding the Phoenix has been passed down to us through the millennia as in the form of the *May*-pole, when during this month our ancestors sacrificed a victim to placate the gods.(13) This was conducted to thwart disaster and the fact that it was a ceremony only conducted in May is quite prophetic. It was at this time that Beltane was celebrated widely throughout Celtdom, a festival surviving today in Irish tradition that acknowledges the god of *death*.

As 1687 BC was the end of the Archaic Civilization and the Children of the Sun 552 years after the Great Flood in 2239 BC, counting another 552 years brings us to 1135 BC when Phoenix transited and darkened the sun again. This was during the reign of Nebuchadnezzar I of Babylon and an ancient Babylonian tablet in the British Museum [BM 40085] from this period reads, "If on the first day of the month of Nisan [April-May] the *sun looks sprinkled with blood* and the light is cool: the king will die and there will be mourning in the country."(14) This seems to be quite prophetic against the Egyptians. In this year King Sethnahkt founded the 20th Dynasty over Egypt and immediately died right before a terrifying omen – an immense black cloud covered the sky and the *sun turned blood red and disappeared*. Day became night and a rain of dust blanketed the land.(15) This same blanketing of dust was recorded all around the world in 1902 AD when Phoenix silently passed through the inner solar system unseen from earth.

The greatest evidence that astronomical knowledge of planet Phoenix was a Bronze Age science is found in Robert Graves's research in *The Greek Myths* on page 412. He records a startling tradition concerning two brothers who contended over the right to rule the Argives of Mycenae. Graves dates this episode as occurring before 1050 BC and after the Trojan War. As Graves notes elsewhere that he believed the Trojan War occurred around 1184 BC (it did not, having occurred in 1229 BC), we find that he dated the following story as happening during this 134 year window of time. The story goes that one of the brothers, named Atreus, who was an astronomer, predicted the exact time when the sun would darken. The tradition is very specific that his method of interpretation was *mathematical*. When the time came and the *sun darkened*, proving his calculation correct, Atreus was declared the leader of the Argives and his brother departed. Graves remarks that Socrates took this tradition very seriously, regarding it as evidence in his own theory that there are cycles of vast duration that result in *destructions*. This means that Socrates believed that Atreus merely deduced the timing when the sun darkened by calculating it from those times it was recorded to darken before. Unfortunately, modern historians always refer to stories like this as evidence of *eclipses*, which are so much more difficult to predict because the shadow of the moon is so small on the earth as opposed to the earth-swallowing shadow of Phoenix. That Atreus predicted the sun-darkening event in 1135 BC is chronologically sound, for shortly afterward the Dorian invasion plunged all of ancient Greece into a Dark Age. The Atreus account further supports the fact that Thales of Miletus had access to ancient astronomical chronologies of Phoenix for he accurately predicted the darkening of the sun in 583 BC exactly 552 years later, as seen in *When the Sun Darkens*.

Phoenix orbited and returned 138 years later in 997 BC. In this year King David, who ruled over the Israelites, was 42 years old. He led a series of battles against the Philistines and preserved current events in many of his Psalms. A passage attributed to David in the Book of 2 Samuel reads:

> The earth shook and trembled; the founda-
> tions of heaven moved and shook, because
> He was wroth. There went out a smoke out
> of his nostrils, and fire out of his mouth de-
> voured . . . He bowed the heavens also, and
> *darkness* was under his feet. And He rode
> upon a cherub, and did fly, He was seen upon
> the wings of the wind. And He made dark-
> ness pavilions round about Him, dark waters,
> and *thick clouds of the skies*. The Lord thun-
> dered from heaven and the Most High uttered
> His voice. And He sent out arrows, and scat-
> tered them, and lightnings. . ."

In antiquity the world was considered the footstool of God, so when it was stated that darkness was under His feet, it meant that the *world had darkened*. The old Semitic peoples, Assyrians, Babylonians and their predecessors the Akkadians all represented Phoenix as a winged disk, sometimes blackened out and sometimes with a small deity riding it. This is the image David provides by describing God upon a *cherub*. The Israelites looked into the heavens and saw the immense planetary body fly by, blackening out the sun, causing electromagnetic storms, quakes and falling stars while blanketing the earth in debris. They quite naturally associated the unbelievable sight with the appearance of their God. In another Old Testament record in 1 Chronicles 21:16, just prior to a battle with the Philistines David looked into the heavens and saw the Angel of Death between heaven and earth like a *sword* over Jerusalem. The imagery of a sword is used in Genesis also when describing the *fiery flaming cherub* with a *flaming sword* that blocked man's access back into Eden, which readers of *When the Sun Darkens* will know occurred in 3895 BC – precisely in conjunction with a Phoenix appearance.

This was not the beginning of mankind, but the beginning of a very important *calendar* adopted by ancient men. As Phoenix brought nothing but chaos and destruction, the appellation "Angel of Death" was rather appropriate.

Joseph in *Survivors of Atlantis* contributed to this thesis unknowingly when he cited the findings of scientists who claim that at approximately 1000 BC (3 years variance) a locally catastrophic impact devastated the badlands of northern Montana.(16) Phoenix departed the inner system and 138 years later returned in 859 BC during the reign of Shalmaneser III of Assyria. During this time Israel was ruled by the infamous queen Jezebel from Phoenicia, who had become queen of Samaria. She hated Elijah the prophet and sought, on more than one occasion, to kill him. Elijah the prophet challenged the prophets of Baal and his dry sacrifice was incinerated by a mysterious fire from heaven, which was followed days later by an earthquake.(17) In the Scriptures Elijah being taken up into heaven is a strange parallel of what happened to Enoch before the Flood. Both prophets are associated with Phoenix.

Phoenix returns again 138 years later in 721 BC when Shalmaneser V of Assyria was ruling and carried away the Israelites into captivity. After an extended siege of Samaria the Israelites were crushed, enslaved and deported to the east. Though this was a major event in biblical history this author was disturbed that he could find no records of the appearance of Phoenix in this year. Naturally the Israelites would not have recorded the event as they were in turmoil and chains. But having now reviewed the writings of Augustine, it is now clear that there is a record of such an event.

Citing again from Marcus Varro's history of the Roman people, Augustine relates that toward the end of Romulus's reign over Rome, the *sun darkened*. . . and Augustine makes sure that we know it was not an eclipse caused by the moon. He wrote, ". . .for it is sufficiently demonstrated that this later obscuration of the sun did not occur by the natural laws of the heavenly bodies." This admits the darkening was not by the moon. Other ancient writers ". . .speak not of an eclipse but of a sudden storm. . ."(18) This Phoenix transit that blackened the sun occurred in the 32nd year of the reign of Romulus, toward the end of his reign.

Planet Phoenix continued on its 138-year orbit and returned in 583 BC, the most well documented of all of the evidences shown in *When the Sun Darkens* – a darkening of the sun actually *predicted* by Thales of Miletus.

In the record of Herodotus is a battle between the Medes and Lydians that was stopped in mid-career because the sun mysteriously darkened and terrified both armies, who then concluded a peace treaty. A rock inscription from 583 BC at Yazilikaya in Asia Minor is believed by Immanuel Velikovsky to be a memorial of this truce. The king of Media, Cyaxeres, with king Nabopolasser of Babylon, conquered Nineveh of the Assyrians, resulting later in the fall of the Assyrian Empire. Babylon took preeminence and then fought a war against the Lydians, which ended before the 583 BC episode. The peace settlement was negotiated between Media and Lydia through a king of Babylon who Velikovsky is convinced was *Nebuchadnezzar II* in his *Ages in Chaos*. This was the king of Babylon who destroyed Jerusalem just two years earlier. The scholar Velikovsky noticed that upon the monument describing this truce the kings of Media and Lydia stand together holding up an *eclipsed sun*. This controversial historian also found an inscription from the same time of a King Mursilis, which reads, "While I marched toward the land Azzi, the *sun became obscured*."(19)

At this time in the Far East another calendar was born. In 583 BC the first Emperor of Japan began his rule in this year according to the Nihon Shoki [Chronicle of Japan], beginning the Japanese regnal lists.(20) At this time there seems to be a revival of the Sons of the Sun traditions in the east. It was also an Asian custom to begin a newer dynasty overthrowing the older ones when any disaster afflicted the land, considering this to be the Mandate of Heaven.

The darkenings of the sun that terrified the ancients in 2239 BC, 1687 BC, 1135 BC and 583 BC are the foundations to the universal traditions of the Four Suns, or Four Ages of mankind. Each one of these Phoenix transits was 552 years apart, or 4 orbits of Phoenix at 138 years each. This period of time in world history encompassed exactly *1656 years* [552 x 3] – from the Great Flood in 2239 BC to the sun-darkening of 583 BC, stopping the Medes and Lydians. This 1656-year period mirrors the *1656 years* that counted down to the Deluge, for as we have seen, the Great Flood was dated by the ancients as occurring in the 1656th year of the Old World's calendar. This means that the Great Flood of 2239 BC was a major Old Bronze Age Isometric Epicenter marking the conjunction of two 1656 year periods going backward and forward in time, a 3312 year period beginning in 3895 BC and ending in 583 BC.

This chronological revelation is made all the more profound by this author's discovery that the independent writer and chronologist Stephen Jones claimed *3895 BC* as Year One on the Ancient World's calendar, which was a date he arrived at after conducting an extensive study of biblical passages, the *Book of Jasher's* chronological references and the Assyrian records. His work is filled with chronological data and charts and is entitled *Secrets of Time*, a monumental work of genius. That the beginning of this grand isometric projection was the start of the original Hebrew Calendar [before corruption by rabbinical torture of older texts] would now imply that the *end* of this timeline would have some significance to the Phoenix, for Phoenix visitations to the inner system are the absolute foundation to biblical chronology.

The year 583 BC, which ends this 3312-year period [1656 + 1656], was exactly 24 orbits of Phoenix, which reappears every 138 years. However, this year ended the Age of the Phoenix. Four darkenings of the sun – 2239, 1687, 1135 and 583 BC were remembered by the ancients as the Four Sun Ages, immortalized upon the Aztec *Stone of the Fifth Sun,* excavated by the Spanish in 1790 AD. Known also as the Calendar Stone, this 20-ton relic depicts four distinct historical disasters caused or linked to the sun, but also *predicts* a fifth cataclysm involving the sun. The relic is adorned with images of earthquakes, comets and destruction. The Age of the Phoenix came to an end at this time because it failed to visually appear at the appointed time. Our predecessors kept track of the Phoenix Cycles, knowing that it reappeared to darken the sun every 552 years. In *When the Sun Darkens* we find evidence that at certain years the Assyrians expected its appearance and the Babylonians renamed their kings in honor of Phoenix reappearances. Remember, Thales of Miletus predicted and published widely the news of the darkening of the sun in 585 BC, claiming that it would occur in *two years* (583 BC).

The next scheduled appearance should have been in 31 BC but the sun did not darken. This was the final date inscribed upon an Olmec date-stele and it was the year of the famous Battle of Actium between Marc Antony and Cleopatra's combined Roman and Egyptian-Greek forces against Octavian. During this battle a major earthquake afflicted Greece and Judea, evidence of the powerful mass of Phoenix passing close by, but invisible in the daytime because it did not transit between earth and the sun.

Though the Legend of the Phoenix died out at this time the scientific records did not. At about this same time the philosopher-naturalist Lucretius wrote a stunning poem over 7300 lines in length and declared that some unknown body, not the moon, *darkens the earth at a fixed time.* Less than a century later the famous Roman writer, geographer and historian, Pliny the Elder, would write that these long, drawn-out eclipses of the sun were mysterious (not caused by the moon), and ". . .their cause was hidden by the rarity of their occurrence." This reminds one of a passage in *Breaking the Godspell* by Neil Freer: "A careful analysis of the historical facts shows that the scholars of ancient times had a great deal more accurate information available to them than most historians have judged and the scientific traditions preceding them were of a much higher level."(21)

Recently while reading a history of the Olympics after *When the Sun Darkens* was released in 2009 this author literally came out of his seat when happening upon a reference to a series of destructive earthquakes that occurred in the year 522 AD. In this year Olympia was ruined and Greece afflicted.(22)   As this was during the Dark Ages, we are fortunate to even have this record. As readers of *Anunnaki Homeworld* will know, the year 522 AD was the ONLY year in world history that both the planet Phoenix *and* the planet NIBIRU entered the inner system on their 138 year and 792 year orbits. These long-period, highly elliptical orbits are fully explained in *Anunnaki Homeworld*. It had bothered this author considerably that he could find no references to evidence of the passage of these planets. What links the quakes to Phoenix so strongly is the fact that this was 552 years after the earthquakes that afflicted the Aegean and Judea in 31 BC. The Phoenix Cycles remain true after 583 BC (though the sun does not always darken) because Phoenix is not in alignment with earth's orbit anymore. 552 years after 583 BC was 31 BC and 552 years after 31 BC was the year 522 AD.

Phoenix can orbit out of planetary alignment so that it passes through the inner system but not in between earth and the sun because Earth is somewhere else on its orbital path around the sun. As a result, Phoenix falls out of memory. Men forget about the Legend of the Phoenix and the 552-year cycle is no longer remembered because it lacks relevance. The planet Phoenix was not seen again until 1764 AD when the astronomer Hoffman witnessed a dark circle obscure one-fifth of the sun's surface through a telescope in the month of May. Many people all over Europe looked up and saw this obscuration with the naked eye. This partial transit is indicative that the Phoenix object was beginning to realign with its historic and *apocalyptic* orbital cycle. 522 AD was *1242 years* before 1764 AD, or 9 orbits of Phoenix at 138 years each.

In Nostradamus' *Letter to King Henry* of France he relates that in his pre-flood chronological studies that he found that there was *1242 years* from Adam to Noah.(23) This arbitrary sum is too specific to ignore. It reveals that there were historical chronologies available to the prophet that have since been lost. He described 9 orbits of Phoenix (1242 years). The sum of 1242 years is exactly half that of 2484 years, which was the duration of time, according to the ancient Greek naturalist Aristarchus, that occurred *between catastrophes*. These men had access to chronological records we no longer possess. Nostradamus was Catholic by necessity – the religion imposed upon his Jewish parents. The Israelites long ago were aware of the 138-year orbit of Phoenix and so were the Egyptians as shown in *When the Sun Darkens*. We know that Nostradamus received a private education from the elders of his

Jewish community before he left on his own for academic training. In a letter written by Nostradamus to his son Cesar, translated by Carlo Patrian, we learn that Nostradamus was privy to various historical and prophetic volumes that had been hidden for centuries.(24) We are also aware that the prophet was a student of the chronological research of the scholar Trithemius, whose own work was published in 1522 AD.(25)

As 1764 AD saw the realigning of planet Phoenix to transit between earth and the sun, and counting 138 years later we arrive at 1902 AD, when our planet passed through an immense strewn field of debris and the entire world was blanketed in dust and mud. The year before, in 1901, the Cincinnati Astral Society published a prediction that a new comet would appear soon and that it orbited an *unknown planet*. One year later in 1902 astronomers discovered comet Morehouse and admitted that it orbits not the sun, but some other body.

Nostradamus historian David Ovason in his *The Secret of Nostradamus* wrote that the prophet employed the lunar timeline of Trithemius in Quatrain I:48 which reads, ". . .the sun will take the remaining days. . . and then is accomplished the end of my prophecy."(26) Ovason believes that this Quatrain pinpointed the year 1901 AD as beginning the *last days of the sun*. The sun is the center of all our calendrical systems. It is my belief that the prophet actually targeted the year 1902. And this would have remained simply as wishful conjecture had it not been for the amazing discovery of another Nostradamus text. In 1994 members of the Italian National Library in Rome discovered buried in their archives a formerly unknown and unpublished manuscript, fully illustrated with paintings and text personally done by the prophet Nostradamus.

After studying this work the Roman researcher and Nostradamus expert Ottovio Cesare Ramotti published in his book, *Nostradamus: The Lost Manuscript*, the following passage, written by the prophet, which refers to the year 1903.

"Many will die before the Phoenix dies, until six hundred and seventy his dwelling shall endure . . .(27)

Ramotti's timeline could have easily started in 1902 without disrupting his research. The reference to *Phoenix* cannot be understated. As will be shown in this book, the prophet Nostradamus not only knew of the existence of this terrible planet but also knew the exact year of its return. And he was not the only one. Ramotti's research claims that some of the Quatrains are coded, and this passage was decoded from 2:53.

Thus far we can conclude that Nostradamus knew that:

(1)   Phoenix appeared in 1902 to begin its final countdown;

(2)   Phoenix is associated to the sun and moon, therefore it is a celestial body;

(3)   Phoenix is associated to world chronology;

(4)   Phoenix is associated to End-Time prophecies;

(5)   Phoenix is connected to the death of many peoples;

(6)   Phoenix will come to an end.

Now we shall set out to prove just this.

III

The Date-Index of Nostradamus

"In due course of time the future
will be known." —*Nostradamus* (1)

Thousands of books and articles have been published concerning the prophet Nostradamus and his mysterious prophecies. Only one of these books that this author has found actually purports that the French seer *dated* his predictions. Mario Reading in *Nostradamus: The Complete Prophecies for the Future* demonstrates this date-index in a neat chronological format easy to follow. The research of this French translator provides us the exact dates that Nostradamus assigned to his quatrains.

The system is quite simple; it is amazing that someone else before him had not already deciphered this dating system. Nostradamus recorded his prophecies in a book called *Centuries*, not denoting actual one hundred year periods but dividing his predictions into hundred-quatrain sections. Mr. Reading believes that much of the content of the *Centuries* refers to many historical events that unfolded prior to the 21st century AD, but that the French seer was essentially an *end-time* prophet.

Mario Reading shows that the number of the Century has no relevance whatsoever in chronologically dating the quatrains, and nor does the number of the quatrain, for all events preceding the 21st century, beginning with the year 2000 AD. But beginning with the 21st century the quatrains take on a certain pattern and actually identify the precise year of their fulfillment in the Anno Domini calendar. Thus, Century 1/Quatrain 16 would refer specifically to 2016 AD, or Century 5/Quatrain 23 would refer to 2023 AD (these are made-up examples). The Century itself has no chronological significance but the number of the quatrain *is the year itself*.

This is not an untenable theory. Nostradamus claimed that he could have dated all of his prophecies but neglected to do this for reasons only known to him. Further, the Anno Domini dating system was the established calendar in his time and if he dated the future events, even in a code, it would have been using this system. If this theory is true and can be demonstrated then it raises an interesting point not mentioned by Mario Reading – the very old belief that prophecies are generally not to be understood until the epoch of their fulfillment. Prophecies of far-off events have no value and are easily forgotten but are meant to be understood by those generations that are about to suffer the situations of their content.

If Mr. Reading is correct then this implies that for one to understand the future as it will unfold in the 21st century, then one must eliminate all those quatrains that have met fulfillment in the past so that what remains would be those referring to the 21st century, which would be *dated* paralleling the number of the quatrain.

In considering the predictions of the prophet we must keep in mind that Nostradamus was also a chronologist. He also acknowledged that his ability did not derive from himself alone. Writing to his son Cesar he said, ". . .the perfect knowledge of events cannot be acquired without divine inspiration, since all prophetic inspiration receives its principle motivating force from God the Creator.(2) This was written almost four hundred years before Oswald Spengler wrote, "The greatest mathematical thinkers, the creative artists of the realm of numbers, have been brought to their decisive mathematical discoveries of their several cultures by a deep religious intuition."(3)

Mario Reading's work is not better known because he committed an error fatal to his research. Though he discovered the date-index and had a wonderful book published, he also deviated away from his own discovery and applied some quatrains to current events that had nothing to do with the seer's predictions. Many authors writing about the future fall prey to this procedure, seeing in current world events a present reflection of some ancient predictions when in fact they have no relation. Having wandered away from his own discovery, he thought he found quatrains that pertained to the years 2001-2012 AD when in fact the quatrains he cited were numbered [dated] otherwise. The events he had predicted did not transpire, and now, in 2012, his book is largely unknown.

Though the author committed this error, this does not negate the validity of his discovery. In fact, with the year 2016 AD his interpretations of future events based off of the corresponding quatrains in his date-index are perfect. And remarkably, the future Mario Reading sees in the predictions of

Nostradamus from 2016 on through 2046 AD mirror exactly what this author has published in *When the Sun Darkens* and in *Anunnaki Homeworld*. These books are based on extensive astronomical chronologies measuring the orbit of long-period celestial bodies spanning thousands of years of recorded history that Mario Reading does not so much as even hint that he is aware of. These are *fixed* timelines that reveal that our world is going to suffer back-to-back global catastrophes in 2040 and 2046 AD. Mr. Reading made a legitimate discovery, the date-index is real, and it will be shown in this chapter that Nostradamus knew all about these two very terrible years.

The conclusion to *When the Sun Darkens* was that the return of planet Phoenix in 2040 AD is the subject matter of Revelation 6:12-14, better known as the Sixth Seal of the Apocalypse:

> And I beheld when he had opened the sixth
> seal, and lo, there was a great *earthquake*;
> and the *sun became black* as sackcloth of
> hair, and the *moon became as blood*. And the
> stars of heaven fell unto the earth, even as a
> fig tree casteth her untimely figs, when she is
> shaken of a mighty wind. And the *heaven de-*
> *parted as a scroll* when it is rolled together;
> and every mountain and island were *moved*
> *out of their places*.

The last visitation of Phoenix was in 1902 when the earth was blanketed in hundreds of millions of tons of dust and mud starting in May. Also in May the volcano called Mt. Pelee on Martinique exploded, killing all 30,000 people in St. Pierre, save for a single survivor.(4) Volcanic activity goes hand-in-hand with Phoenix visitations throughout history. The Sixth Seal prophecy involves very specific descriptions of a *pole-shift* when the outer lithosphere smoothly glides over the mantle and displaces entire continents, causing oceans to invade coastal lands, extreme seismic disturbances and volcanism.

As seen in the prior chapter it is believed that Nostradamus named the Phoenix and associated it with the year 1903. It is also known that the coat of arms for the family of Nostradamus was a shield with two solar symbols and the head of a *phoenix*. Though Nostradamus was no doubt heavily influenced by his Judeo-Christian [Catholic] background, these are not enough to explain his prophetic precision. He was a self-proclaimed descendant of the Israelite tribe of Issachar(5), and interestingly, if this was true or not, the biblical record states that the men of Issachar were *keepers of the times*.

Employing his date-index, Mario Reading claims that Century 2/Quatrain 40 refers clearly to 2040 AD. His translation reads:

> A short while after a previous occurrence
> a further fierce storm will arise over
> land and sea. The seaborne cost of this one
> will be even larger. Fire, animals, it will
> be even greater. Outrage.

Mr. Reading claims that this is a very literal passage that conveys that some powerfully destructive storm will follow a similarly destructive but less powerful one in 2040. There seems to be a correlation between this quatrain and the Sixth Seal disaster in Revelation, both focusing on the *sea*. Mario Reading curiously does not continue the passage, for the very next quatrain continues the description of what is to occur in 2040.

We now review this connected passage in Erika Cheetham's *The Final Prophecies of Nostradamus*, Century 2/Quatrain 41.

> The great star will burn for seven days
> and the cloud will make the sun appear
> double. The large mastiff will howl all
> night when the great pontiff changes his
> abode.

In 2239 BC the inhabitants of the earth witnessed planet Phoenix for *seven days* before the Great Flood – darkening the sun. The cloud reference further hints to cosmic dust, for the reference to "cloud" is in the singular. Plurality would have denoted mere atmospheric clouds common every day. Some translators prefer to have this passage refer to the appearance of *two suns* rather than the sun appearing double. Phoenix, approaching from a certain angle would appear brilliantly reflecting the sunlight. But the greatest link to the Phoenix pole shift is the statement, ". . .the great pontiff changes his abode." It must be remembered that the quatrains are full of astronomical symbols and metaphors. The "great pontiff" is none other than the sun, which in a pole shift alters its course across our skies, or "changes its abode." It is not the sun moving but the earth turning upside down, with crustal slippage changing terrestrial geography and our vantage point. During the day the sun will veer off course and the day will turn into night in minutes and at night there will be a sudden appearance of the bright sun awakening those lost in sleep.

As shown in *When the Sun Darkens*, the east will be shoved northward while the west [Americas] will be pushed southward; the epicenter of turning [like an axis] will be the Israel-Egypt region. When Graham Hancock published his famous *Fingerprints of the Gods*, the scientific evidence available at that time in the early 1990s revealed that a reversal of earth's magnetic poles was scheduled for about 2030 AD.(6) But since 2006 the magnetic poles had wandered exponentially far from the true poles. It is difficult for scientists to predict such phenomena when they will not admit the fact of rogue planetary bodies of immense size as being part of our own solar system that travel highly elliptical orbits that take them way out in the vast Kuiper Belt.

Nostradamus did not leave so earth-shattering an event within only a couple quatrains. He was much more thorough than that. Several times the prophet encoded the same event or events that occur in one year but spread throughout three or more quatrains. It is the subject matter that links them together. Here is an example of Nostradamus's method:

In Century l/quatrain 43 we read:

> Before the coming of the end of the empire
> a miraculous event will take place. A field
> removed, the pillar of porphyry put in place
> on the gnarled rock.

In Century IX/ quatrain 32 we read:

> A deep column of fine porphyry is found,
> inscriptions of the capitol under the
> base, Bones, twisted hair. The Roman
> strength tried, the fleet is stirred at the
> harbor of Mytylene.

In Century X/quatrain 93 we read:

> The new Barque will go on voyages, far and
> near they will transfer the empire. Beaucaire
> and Arles will retain the hostages, near where
> two columns of porphyry are found.

All three of these quatrains appear in different Centuries. All three mention a column [pillar] or columns of porphyry. These passages refer to some astonishing archeological discovery in the future. The reference to bones and twisted hair is no mystery. Archeologists come across human sacrifices laid beneath ancient foundations and cornerstones of monuments excavated. I would employ Mr. Reading's date-index and assign two of these quatrains to 2032 AD, which would be *before* the end of the empire, which will no doubt come with the disasters of 2040. The third quatrain used the columns of porphyry only for a geographical marker, meaning that the events of that quatrain are later than the discovery of the columns. We will not spend time trying to interpret these quatrains and those they seem to be connected with. These were provided in example to show that Nostradamus would use a quatrain to establish a date and then add other quatrains connected to it through subject matter rather than number designations. This allowed him to elaborate when he needed to because some years would be full of events as opposed to others.

This next example of his method provides us absolute proof that Nostradamus knew about planet Phoenix, describes it, dates its appearance and even encodes its orbital duration of 138 years. . . all in the next four quatrains.

In Century 2/quatrain 43 we read:

> During the appearance of the *bearded star*,
> the three great princes will be made enemies.
> The tremulous peace on earth will be struck
> from the skies; the Po, the winding Tiber,
> a serpent on the shore.

In Century 5/Quatrain 59 we read:

> The English chief stays too long at Nimes
> towards Spain, Aenobarbe to the rescue.
> Many will die through war started on that day
> when a *bearded star* falls in Artois.

In Century 6/quatrain 6 we read:

> He will appear towards the north, not far
> from the *bearded star* in Cancer. Susa, Siene,
> Boetia, Eretria; the great man of Rome will
> die, the night dispersed.

In Century 2/quatrain 15 we read:

> A short while before a king is murdered, Cas-
> tor and Pollux in the ship, a *bearded star*.
> Public treasure plundered on land and sea;
> Pisa, Asti, Terrera and Turin are forbidden
> territories.

The "bearded star" is a phrase the French seer borrowed from Aristotle's *Meteorology*, referring to a celestial body with a tail that stretches in one direction.(7) In fact, the word "comet" derives from roots meaning *hairy star*. These four quatrains in all of Nostradamus's writings are the only references to *bearded stars*, thus linking them all to the same event. Other comets are mentioned in his Centuries but they are not described in this fashion. We pay close attention to Century 6/6 which reads that ". . .the great man of Rome will die," which is a code. The great men of Rome in his days, before and even after, were *pontiffs*. The Papacy of Rome ruled the European courts with an iron fist. The pontiff of Rome as seen in Century 2/41 is a symbol for the *sun*, which changed its abode. This is confirmed as Century 6/6 continues, stating that after the death of the great man of Rome [sun], ". . .*the night dispersed.*" As night is the opposite of day, this describes a pole shift caused by the bearded star, which takes peace from the earth and is the reason why the public treasures [stores and depots] are looted.

These bearded star references are connected by symbols to Century 2/41, which as we have seen is a continuation of Century 2/40, which, in Mario Reading's date-index, is 2040 AD. The reference to Castor and Pollux identifies the time of May-June and the region of Gemini in the sky. At the end of May the sun is in the House of the Twins, according to Robert Graves, scholar of Grecian antiquities. These four "bearded star" quatrains directly refer to planet Phoenix and its affect upon earth, and we have as our proof of this, the mathematical code the prophet left to those who would search for it. He cleverly hid the 138-year orbit of Phoenix within the quatrains themselves.

$$\text{Century 2/ } 43 \ = \ 45$$
$$\text{Century 5/ } 59 \ = \ 64$$
$$\text{Century 6/ } 6 \ = \ 12$$
$$\text{Century 2/ } 15 \ = \ 17$$

By adding each century and quatrain the total is *138*. Because these are the only four passages in all of his prophecies mentioning a "bearded star" then we cannot attribute this to accident. We find more evidence of Nostradamus' chronological genius. He encoded this 138 years in only four quatrains. 138 x 4 is 552 years. . . a Phoenix Cycle. One could accuse this of being too arbitrary or coincidental, so take this into consideration. Nostradamus dictated his *Centuries* to his secretary who wrote them all down for publication in 1553 AD. Mario Reading is convinced that the terminal period of the French Prophet's messages concern the year *2105 AD*, which is exactly 552 years after 1553. Interestingly, the chronological tables in *When the Sun Darkens* demonstrate that a 6000 year countdown began in 3895 BC and ends in 2106 AD, exactly *552 years* after 1554 AD, when all of Europe was afire with the predictions of Michel Nostramdame, aka Nostradamus.

The prophet concealed much more information spread throughout his work concerning 2040 AD. Century 2/40 *dated* the event and the following passage in Century 2/41 supplemented it. The *"bearded star"* passages encode the identity of Phoenix and are filled with subject matter that links them to other obscure quatrains that could only be descriptive of the 2040 AD disasters. Before we explore these amazing passages our attention is turned to one clever date-passage hidden by Nostradamus. In Century 9/quatrain 31 we read:

> The trembling of the earth at Martara,
> the tin island of St. George half sunk.
> Drowsy with peace, war will arise at
> Easter. In the Temple abysses opened.

Erika Cheetham is an Oxford scholar who has studied and written books about Nostradamus and his prophecies. She relates that Martara is 1000 miles away from Britain ["island of St. George"] so this must describe a massive earthquake. It is probable that the half of England that is sunk into the Atlantic Ocean will be the southern half, with London disappearing beneath the waters. As readers of *When the Sun Darkens* will remember, this is also the fate of New York City in 2040, which also lies upon an Atlantic coast.

It must also be mentioned here that the *English* and a *war* are elements found in the "bearded star" passage of Century 5/59. This prophecy in Century 9/31 concerns destruction caused by the sea. The bearded star references in Century 2/43 and 2/15 refer to rivers, the seashore, the sea, the regions of Pisa, Asti, Terrera and Turin becoming forbidden territories [flooded] and they mention Castor and Pollux, the patron gods of the sea and sailors. Our study began with Century 2/40, which describes ruination by water.

But the code of Nostradamus dating Century 9/31 is so simple it was almost missed. Century 9 added to quatrain 31 is *40*, and this satisfies Mario Reading's date-index, identifying 2040 AD as the date when half of England, or the British Isles, will sink below the ocean.

The pole shift and global cataclysm and current events at that time are found in chronological order in quatrains numbered 81, 82, 83, 84, 85, 86, 87 and 88, however, these quatrains are not in the same Century. They are spread throughout the predictions of the prophet but we can easily see the pattern numerically and link them to the 2040 AD disaster by their *content*, which is exactly what Nostradamus wanted the interpreter to do.

Century 8/quatrain 81 reads:

> The new empire in desolation, will be
> changed from the northern pole. From Sicily
> will come such trouble that it will bother the
> enterprise tributary to Philip.

The "new empire" is a prophetic reference to the United States of North America, which did not exist in 1554 when Nostradamus wrote down the Centuries. When referring to nations and empires the prophet clearly identifies them through cultural symbols, geographical descriptions, by their leader's identities or through clearly understood metaphors. In *When the Sun Darkens* we find not only New York destroyed in 2040, but the North American continent is shoved southward, away from the Northern hemisphere, to occupy the regions once known as Mexico and Central America, which are also shoved southward to become the new South America but are heavily destroyed as they pass over the equatorial bulge. South America becomes the New Antarctica while the reverse occurs in the Far East and everything is pushed northwards. In the place of Canada and the USA are the fragmented and broken lands of ice and rock formerly of the Arctic. Erika Cheetham, having never reviewed any data on Phoenix or this author's research believes that this passage refers to a civilization that moves southwards.

Century 1/quatrain 82 reads:

> When even the trees shake mightily and
> the south wind seems covered in blood, so

> many will try to escape that Vienna and all
> Austria will shake with their passing.

The prophet borrows imagery from the Book of Revelation, in fact, from the passage concerning Phoenix, the Sixth Seal, when he wrote, ". . .trees shake mightily," with the biblical text reading, ". . .[fig tree] shaken of a mighty wind." The association on the prophet's part was *deliberate*, linking the sun darkening episode and moon turning to a blood color with this prediction about ". . .the south wind seemed covered in blood." This would indeed be an accurate description, as planet Phoenix will bath the world in cosmic dust that would blanket the earth as it did in 1902. The word phoenix, as translated by Robert Graves, means *blood red*, as found on page 650 of his celebrated *The Greek Myths*. This is Mario Reading's translation of the quatrain. He assigned this to 2082 AD, adhering to his date-index. He was unaware that Nostradamus used some quatrains to establish a date and then connected other quatrains through imagery and association to elaborate on certain important years.

Century 9/quatrain 83 reads:

> . . .a great earthquake will totally destroy
> the packed theatre. Air, sky and earth will
> be murky and unsettled so that even Infidels
> will call on God and the saints to steer them.

This is Mario Reading's translation. Of course the quake, the ruin of architecture and the air being murky are all caused by Phoenix occulting the sun in transit. The language employed here, *to steer them*, links us back with Castor and Pollux guiding the *ship*, or Earth. In a pole shift, direction changes and the former terrestrial geographical markers indicating the cardinal directions no longer point out north, east, south and west. We are unsure how long the planet will wobble before it stabilizes. Before we go on to the next passage we need to revive Erika Cheetham's interpretation of this same Century 9/quatrain 83 text:

> The sun in twenty degrees of Taurus there
> will be a great earthquake. The great theatre,
> full, will be ruined. Darkness and trouble
> in air, sky and land when they call upon the
> faithless God and His saints.

Quite a difference, though the general message remains the same. What is useful to us is the Oxford scholar's commentary that this passage retains precise astronomical data revealing that the quake and darkness occur in *May*. Again, it cannot be overstated, Erika Cheetham knows nothing of planet Phoenix nor its passing through the inner system every 138 years in May.

Century 1/quatrain 84 reads:

> The moon eclipsed in great gloom, his broth-
> er becomes the color of blood. The great one,
> hidden for a long time in the shadows, will
> hold a blade in the bloody wound.

Herein Nostradamus still describes the Phoenix transit. The brother of this darkened moon is the *sun*, which is perfectly in accord with the ancient view that the moon was feminine and the sun masculine. The "great one" is again a reference to the sun, linking this quatrain to Century 2/41 where ". . .the great pontiff changes his abode." This *great one* is the "great man of Rome [pontiff: sun]" in Century 6/6 when the night disperses. He is "hidden for a long time in the shadows." The reference to a *blade* parallels the Genesis description of the "fiery flaming sword" that appeared in 3895 BC and deterred mankind from traveling back eastward toward Eden. Which was Phoenix.

These quatrains reviewed number 81, 82, 83, 84, spread throughout different Centuries. Because of their direct relevance to our thesis, we will now review quatrains numbered 87 and 88.

Century 1/quatrain 87 reads:

> Earthshaking fire from the center of the earth
> will cause tremors around the New City. Two
> great immovable powers will war for a long
> time, then Arethusa will redden a new river.

Nostradamus here veils his subject matter cleverly in astronomical garb. The "two great immovable powers" are the *sun* and *moon* and the image of them at war describes strange sights that will be seen from the surface of the earth as people gaze into the heavens, witnessing these events. It is Phoenix (blood red) that wars against the sun by darkening it and against the moon by turning it the color of blood. Arethusa is mentioned here, a name pulled out of ancient Greek mythology, a daughter of the sea god Poseidon. Because she was turned into a perpetual spring, we see here that Nostradamus is indirectly referring to a *flooding*. The "new river" the prophet wrote of, by this author's own personal interpretation, is the *Hudson River* in North America.

Ordinarily, Nostradamus is very specific with place-names, nationalities and geography. His reference to the New Empire in Century 8/81 was as vague as this above reference to New City. Because these are found within passages all revealing the events of the year 2040, then we are left to believe that the prophet was seeing an empire not known in his day and a major city not known in his day, but ones that would be known *worldwide* by the time of the fulfillment of the prophecy. These are no doubt the United States and the city of New York, both of which are going to be ruined in 2040. We will review another quatrain involving this "New City" before the end of this chapter.

Century 6/ quatrain 88 reads:

> A great kingdom will remain desolate. Near
> the Ebro they will be gathered in assemblies.
> The Pyrenean mountains will console him
> when in *May* there will be earth tremors.

Nostradamus wrote that "the new empire in desolation," in Century 8/81, will be changed from the northern pole. Here he writes ". . .a great kingdom will remain *desolate*." The two are one. Proving this is found in that the tributary of Philip was the country of Spain [Century 8/81], but here we find a reference to the Ebro, a river in Spain. This is the second reference Nostradamus makes to the month of May, both linked to earthquakes. The desolate empire/kingdom and the Spain/Ebro associations connect this passage to those of the "bearded star." In fact, so insistent upon the timing of this 2040 AD series of disasters was the French seer that he mentions the month of May a *third* time.

Century 10/quatrain 67 reads:

> A very great troubling in the month of *May*,
> Saturn in Capricorn, Jupiter and Mercury in
> Taurus. Venus also in Cancer, Mars in Virgo,
> then hail will fall greater than an egg.

With this quatrain we better understand what it conveyed in Century 6/6 concerning the bearded star. It reads, "He will appear towards the north, not far from the bearded star in *Cancer*. . ." This passage mirrors the other concerning Cancer and is an astronomical description of the approach of planet Phoenix from the *north*, above the sun, on its north-to-south passing over the ecliptic where can be seen all of these planetary conjunctions mentioned by Nostradamus. It was the European astronomer Hoffman that in 1764 observed Phoenix pass over the ecliptic from the north traveling south.

Our final 2040 AD passage refers again to the New City, and Erika Cheetham also believes that this is a reference to New York City.

Century 6/quatrain 97 we read:

> The sky will burn at forty-five degrees.
> Fire approaches the great New City. Imme-
> diately a huge scattered flame leaps up when
> they want to have proof of the Normans.

For reasons independent of this study, *When the Sun Darkens* provides data on why this author believes that New York City and much of the east coast will be completely destroyed in the pole shift of 2040 AD. To find these references in the prophecies of Nostradamus merely confirms this belief. Connected to the reference to the New City in Century 1/87, this passage is then linked to those all descriptive of 2040.

The catastrophe of 2040 AD is *not* the beginning of the Apocalypse, and this is why we should be worried. It is the *Sixth* Seal. As the sixth seal pole shift and transit of Phoenix will occur in 2040, a fixed time, then the events of the other seals would occur before this disaster. International wars, global plagues, epidemic and famine. Phoenix will virtually end our technological civilization of comforts, ready-made foods and sanitation while also altering the geographical boundaries of the world as entire nations vanish and others are born out of the chaos.

But this is not the end of the tragedy. Six years later in 2046 AD another ancient planetary body called NIBIRU by the Sumerians and known by many other archaic civilizations will nearly collide into our world and initiate a far worse series of worldwide catastrophes. The French-Jewish prophet did not fail us in reporting this episode either. Employing the date-index discovered by Mario Reading, we discover two quatrains that depict the horrific events of 2046.

Century 2/quatrain 46 reads:

> Following one great human tragedy, a greater
> lies in wait. The mighty movement of the
> centuries begins renewal. Rain, blood, milk,

> famine, sword and the plague. Fire will be
> seen in the sky, with a trail of sparks.

The subject of 2046 AD is fully detailed with extensive charts and data in *Anunnaki Homeworld*. The seer is very adamant in revealing to us that this occurs *after* "one great human tragedy," which is of course the 2040 cataclysm. Cheetham's translation has it as ". . .the great cycle of the centuries is renewed." This is only comprehended in light of the alarming prophecies of the Revelation text, the books of Enoch and evidence in *Anunnaki Homeworld*, revealing that NIBIRU's approach and proximity will push Earth off its orbital path around the sun into a *tighter* orbit that shrinks the year from 365.25 days to a period of *240 days*. This new orbit will initiate a new calendar, or "cycle of the centuries."

In Century 1/quatrain 46 we read:

> Very near Auch, Lectoure and Mirande a
> great fire will fall from the sky for three
> nights. The cause will appear both stupefying
> and marvelous; shortly afterwards there will
> be an earthquake.

The 2046 AD cataclysm is not an extensive subject in the prophecies of Nostradamus. He concentrates on describing the events of 2040, and for good reason. There is a fundamental difference between these two apocalyptic destructions of the world caused by planets Phoenix and NIBIRU. The first planet approaches Earth and completely ends its technologically advanced, global communications networks, from satellites to relay towers to the people that operated them. Power grids go offline, cities vanish, new landmasses appear and a quarter of the world's population dies. As the survivors revert back to tribalism, barbarity and the basic instincts of survival, the second planet approaches and *re-destroys* a world already in ruin. The second planetary cataclysm largely kills off 50% of humanity six years after 25% of mankind was killed. As the epicenter of pole shift rotation and being the regions left largely unaffected in 2040 and 2046 AD, Israel, Iraq and Egypt are the most civilized areas in the world. As news of this spreads, the survivors from around the globe begin their migrations just after 2046. They will be heading toward a new kind of civilization, one ruled by a figure known in the biblical literature and in the prophecies of Nostradamus as the Antichrist. But this is the subject for another book.

Before concluding this chapter there is one additional piece of information connected to this removal of Earth from her present position orbiting the sun that was not mentioned in *Anunnaki Homeworld*. We know that David Davidson, an engineer, studied the complex architectural geometry of the Great Pyramid and came to the stunning conclusion that it encodes an astronomical chronology that *ends* in 2045 AD. This much was mentioned in the prior work. Davidson's research was published in 1924 but he never speculated as to what would transpire at the end of this astronomical chronology. Now, when asked about the Great Pyramid in 1932 the unusual man known as The Sleeping Prophet, the famous Edgar Cayce, in Reading 5748-5 replied:

> ". . .received [the Great Pyramid] all the
> records from the beginning of that given
> by the priests. . . to that period when there
> is to be a *change in earth's position.*"(8)

Previously we saw how the Italian Nostradamus expert Ramotti published a work about a lost manuscript of the prophet Nostradamus and showed how it revealed that the French seer *named* Phoenix in a code that was linked to the year 1903. This manuscript, found in the Italian National Library was used to decode a hidden message in Century 1/quatrain 48 that Ramotti published as saying:

> ". . .the senseless people will be
> reawakened by Jesus from their illusions. . .
> six lenses and a telescope. And I have a true
> key which is even more important to pass
> down. I see coming in my dreams heavy leg-
> ends, receiving the wave of the sun. The Law
> of the Wolves is there to lay blame when it
> is foreseen that the *whole Western World will
> die.* . . I shall know *different times.*"(9)

It has now been demonstrated that Mario Reading's date-index is legitimate and supported by the independent research of this author in *When the Sun Darkens* and *Anunnaki Homeworld*. Nostradamus focused on the terrible date of 2040 but mentioned little of 2046.

He is not alone. Now we shall learn of another seer. She too long ago recorded her prophecies and placed the most emphasis on the *first* cataclysm. But she very specifically details them both.

IV

The Sky-Dragons of 2040 and 2046 AD

"All nature is a gallery of arcana revealing great
truths to those who can decipher them."
—*Thomas Troward, 1902* (1)

In the year 1488 AD a witch in England named Agatha Southeil (variously
spelt as Southill or Sontheil) gave birth to a baby girl she named Ursula.
Ursula grew up to be overly large and was an exceedingly ugly woman. But
she had a gift. Her fame spread across the country as news spread about her
penetrating insight and wisdom. It was said that she could see the future and
as a grown woman she had earned the title of Northern Prophetess.(2)

The year of Ursula Southheil's birth was astronomically unique, for in
1488 the planet Phoenix on its silent 138-year orbit passed through the inner
system, probably unseen from earth. This year was exactly 552 years before
2040 AD, a Phoenix Cycle. Ordinarily this would be unimportant, however it
will herein be shown that her predictions about the future have everything to
do with this largely unknown planetary body.

She was born 15 years before the prophet Nostradamus, who entered
this world in 1503. While she was English and uneducated, he was a French
scholar and doctor of Jewish pedigree. Both were alive and recording their
prophecies at the same time. Ursula Southeil is better known as the famous
Mother Shipton.

She lived for 73 years, dying in 1561 when Nostradamus was 58 years
old. This year is remembered for a strange astronomical occurrence recorded
in Nuremburg, Germany when people looked into the heavens and beheld
a great mass of objects passing over the sun, filling the sky. Among these

objects was a gigantic black, spear-shaped mass that crossed over the surface of the sun(3), similar to a transit by Phoenix, though this body was unknown. Her dire prophecies, as we will see, were very elaborate and specific and were known as the Yorkshire Prophecies, which connects us to an interesting coincidence. In the year she died the famous Sir Francis Bacon was born, at *York* House, London, the son of the Keeper of the Great Seal for the Queen of England.(4)

Though no mention of Mother Shipton is made in any texts prior to 1641(5), in 1740 a John Tyrrel wrote a book about her entitled *Past, Present and to Come: or, Mother Shipton's Yorkshire Prophecy*. The birth-year of 1488 and future messages of the Northern Prophetess from Yorkshire concerning the destruction wrought by Phoenix lends credit to this author's theory, expounded in *When the Sun Darkens*, that New York City is fated to be totally destroyed in 2040.

Her prophecy concerns man's judgment in the Last Days, disasters and plagues caused by the *sixth visitation of the Sky Dragon* to earth.(6)   Her birth in 1488 was 552 years before the *Sixth* Seal of the Apocalypse, which describes the Phoenix transit. As does the French prophet, Mother Shipton accurately saw two global destructions occur back-to-back and these dates are fixed and unchangeable. While Mother Shipton saw more clearly what was going to happen in both interplanetary cataclysms, Nostradamus saw *when*.

Now we shall review her amazing prophecies. The lines of text are numbered by this author to more easily reference them after the poem is reviewed.

The Yorkshire Prophecy

1. And now a word, in uncouth rhyme
2. of what whall be in future time
3. Then upside down the world shall be
4. And gold found at the root of tree
5. All England's sons that plow the land
6. shall oft be seen with book in hand
7. The poor shall now great wisdom know
8. Great houses stand in far flung vale
9. All covered o'er with snow and hail
10. A carriage without horse will go
11. Disaster fill the world with woe.

12. In London, Primrose Hill shall be
13. In centre hold a Bishop's See
14. Around the world men's thoughts will fly
15. Quick as the twinkling of an eye.
16. And water shall great wonders do
17. How strange. And yet it shall come true.
18. Through towering hills proud men shall ride
19. No horse or ass move by his side.
20. Beneath the water, men shall walk
21. Shall ride, shall sleep, shall even talk.
22. And in the air men shall be seen
23. In white and black and even green
24. A great man then, shall come and go
25. For prophecy declares it so.
26. In water, iron, then shall float
27. As easy as a wooden boat
28. Gold shall be seen in stream and stone
29. In land that is yet unknown.
30. And England shall admit a Jew
31. You think this strange, but it is true
32. The Jew that once was held in scorn
33. Shall of a Christian then be born
34. A house of glass shall come to pass
35. In England, but Alas, alas
36. A war will follow with the work
37. Where dwells the Pagan and the Turk
38. These states will lock in fiercest strife
39. And seek to take each other's life.
40. When North shall thus divide the south
41. And Eagle build in Lion's mouth
42. Then tax and blood and cruel war
43. Shall come to every humble door.
44. Three times shall lovely sunny France
45. Be led to play a bloody dance
46. Before the people shall be free
47. Three tyrant rulers shall she see.
48. Three rulers in succession be
49. Each springs from different dynasty.
50. Then when the fiercest strife is done
51. England and France shall be as one.

52. The British olive shall next then twine
53. In marriage with a German vine.
54. Men walk beneath and over streams
55. Fulfilled shall be their wondrous dreams.
56. For in those wondrous far off days
57. The women shall adopt a craze
58. To dress like men, and trousers wear
59. And to cut off their locks of hair
60. They'll ride astride with brazen brow
61. As witches do on broomstick now.
62. And roaring monsters with man atop
63. Does seem to eat the verdant crop
64. And men shall fly as birds do now
65. And give away the horse and plough.
66. There'll be a sign for all to see
67. Be sure that it will certain be.
68. Then love shall die and marriage cease
69. And nations wane as babes decrease
70. And wives shall fondle cats and dogs
71. And men live much the same as hogs.
72. In nineteen hundred and twenty six
73. Build houses light of straw and sticks.
74. For then shall mighty wars be planned
75. And fire and sword shall sweep the land.
76. When pictures seem alive with movements free
77. When boats like fishes swim beneath the sea,
78. When men like birds shall scour the sky
79. Then half the world, deep drenched in blood shall die.
80. For those who live the century through
81. In fear and trembling this shall do.
82. Flee to the mountains and the dens
83. To bog and forest and wild fens.
84. For storms will rage and oceans roar
85. When Gabriel stands on sea and shore
86. And he blows his wondrous horn
87. Old worlds die and new be born.
88. A fiery dragon will cross the sky
89. Six times before this earth shall die
90. Mankind will tremble and frightened be
91. For the SIXTH HERALDS IN THIS PROPHECY.
    [emphasis added]

92. For seven days and seven nights
93. Man will watch this awesome sight.
94. The tides will rise beyond their ken
95. To bite away the shores and then
96. The mountains will begin to roar
97. And earthquakes split the plain to shore.
98. And flooding waters, rushing in
99. Will flood the lands with such a din
100. That mankind cowers in muddy fen
101. And snarls about his fellow men.
102. He bares his teeth and fights and kills
103. And secretes food in secret hills
104. And ugly in his fear, he lies
105. To kill marauders, thieves and spies.
106. Man flees in terror from the floods
107. And kills, and rapes and lies in blood
108. And spilling blood by mankind's hands
109. Will stain and bitter many lands.
110. And when the dragon's tail is gone,
111. Man forgets, and smiles, and carried on
112. To apply himself-too late, too late
113. For mankind has earned deserved fate.
114. His masked smile-his false grandeur,
115. Will serve the Gods their anger stir.
116. And they will send the Dragon back
117. To light the sky-his tail will crack
118. Upon the earth and rend the earth
119. And man shall flee, lord and serf.
120. But slowly they are routed out
121. To seek diminishing water spout
122. And men will die of thirst before
123. The oceans rise to mount the shore.
124. And lands will crack and rend anew
125. You think it strange. It will come true.
126. And in some far off distant land
127. Some men-of such a tiny band
128. Will have to leave their solid mount
129. And span the earth, those few to count,
130. Who survives this [unreadable] and then
131. Begin the human race again.
132. But not on land already there

133. But on ocean beds, stark, dry and bare
134. Not every soul on earth will die
135. As the Dragon's Tail goes sweeping by.
136. Not every land on earth will sink
137. But these will wallow in stench and stink
138. Of rotting bodies of beasts and man
139. Of vegetation crisped on land.
140. But the land that rises from the sea
141. Will be dry and clean and soft and free
142. Of mankind's dirt and therefore be
143. The source of man's new dynasty.
144. And those that live will ever fear
145. The dragon's tail for many year
146. But time erases memory
147. You think it strange. But it will be.
148. And before the race is built anew
149. A silver serpent comes to view
150. And spew out men of like unknown
151. To mingle with the earth now grown
152. Cold from its heat and these men can
153. Enlighten the minds of future man.
154. To intermingle and show them how
155. To live and love and thus endow
156. The children with the second sight
157. A natural thing so that they might
158. Grow graceful, humble and when they do
159. The Golden Age will start anew.
160. The dragon's tail is but a sign
161. For mankind's fall and man's decline.
162. And before this prophecy is done
163. I shall be burned at the stake, at one
164. My body singed and my soul set free
165. You think I utter blasphemy
166. You're wrong. These things have come to me
167. This prophecy will come to be.

These 167 lines of text contain definitive particulars about events that transpired long after Ursula Southeil died. An entire book could be written about the Yorkshire Prophecy and its fulfillment thus far, but herein this author will cover only the more obvious revelations.

Mother Shipton witnessed "a future time," [line 2]. It would have been amazing to her to have seen the explosion of literacy in the 1600s that occurred after her death with the publishing of Bibles in English and the Authorized King James Version in 1611 [lines 5-7]. Automobiles are carriages without horses [line 10]. The reference to a Bishop's See concerns the birth of the Anglican Church in England, born when the king of England officially broke away from the Church of Rome. It was a scandal that shocked the courts of Europe [line 13]. Trains also could be described as carriages without horses and lines 14-15 describe telecommunications around the world, the telegraph, telephone and radio. Hydro-based engineering and technology [lines 16-17] tunneled through hills and mountains for mass-transit, submarines and aircraft are depicted by her in lines 18-23. To Mother Shipton it was almost unbelievable that ships made of *iron* would float [lines 26-27].

As the descendants of the English people through colonial programs gave rise to the Anglo-Saxon population in America, she also predicts many things that were to happen there. In lines 28-29: "Gold shall be seen in stream and stone, in *land that is yet unknown.*" She had died 46 years before Jamestown was founded in North America. This gold just lying around refers to two major discoveries that initiated an increase in European migration to the west. The California Gold Rush of 1849 was 288 years (Golden Proportion number) after her death and this episode was followed shortly afterward by the Klondike Gold Rush of the Yukon, Alaska region.

Another specific historical event concerns lines 30-33. In 1290 AD King Edward I of England enacted the Edict of Expulsion, forcing all Jews to leave England, declaring that any Jews remaining after November 1 would be promptly executed. In Ursula Southeil's day there were no Jews living in her country, Puritanism having strong roots in England. It was felt that as killers of the Christ, the Jews were a cursed race. The status quo was anti-Semitic. In 1649 King Charles I was beheaded at the behest of Oliver Cromwell, a move backed by Parliament for treason.(7) Cromwell received a visit from the leader of the Jewish community of Amsterdam on the Continent in Holland [Amsterdam being the original name of New York City] named Menasseh ben Israel.(8) Cromwell permitted the Jews to return to England, reversing the expulsion act – events which occurred 88 years *after* Mother Shipton's death. She may have been even more specific than this. In 1858 the British government for the *first* time waived the Oath of Parliament when admitting the Jew, Lionel Rothschild, a seat because he refused to swear on the Christian Bible.(9) He was followed by another prominent British official named Benjamin Disraeli, who became Prime Minister of England.

The House of Glass in England, mentioned in lines 34-35, is a stunning reference to the world-renowned Crystal Palace, finished in 1851, or 290 years after Mother Shipton's death. Inside the glass walls that fascinated all visitors from around the globe the English hosted the first World's Fair where technological and engineering advancements were on display. This is followed by lines 36-37 that concern the well-attested wars between the Turks and British, both naval and over land. In lines 38-43 is a description of the American War for Independence from Britain, the "states" being the 13 Colonies. Interestingly, taxation is mentioned and America is symbolized by the Eagle, as Britain is the Lion, two very ancient symbols also found in the biblical prophetic records and apocryphal writings of Esdras. The Eagle always derived from the Lion, as the Americans were descended from [or broke away from] the British. Mother Shipton's prediction continues in historical sequence, for lines 44-51 clearly describe the Napoleonic Wars and the French Revolution that all came on the tail of the American Revolution. The British and French fought one another for centuries and after the revolution in France during the 19th century, the French and British healed their old wounds and are even today staunch allies. Historically, the nobility and dynasties of France and England had intermarried and later this intermarriage included the Prussian, Austrian and German royalty as inferred in lines 52-53.

Next, our Northern Prophetess clearly envisions the *Roaring Twenties* and beyond into the rest of the 20th Century, as the mode of feminine hairstyles and dress is drastically altered [lines 58-59]. In the Dark and Middle Ages up to the time of Ursula Southeil it was considered scandalous for a woman to sit astride a beast like a man does, the social norm enforcing an etiquette requiring women upon horses and mules to sit sideways to keep their legs together [lines 60-61]. This sitting astride a beast was what made the imagery in the Book of Revelation appear more unholy when the Woman sat upon the Scarlet Beast.

Lines 62-71 depict the labor of men being replaced by inventions, great tractors harvesting crops and aircraft that allow men to rely less and less on beasts of burden. With the Industrial Revolution came the initiation of 12 and 14 hour work days in the large cities, the decrease of social interaction, and widespread manufacturing as population centered upon the urban areas. This technological age saw a decline in morality, social fraternities became increasingly superficial and the unity of the family was damaged, becoming a more antiquated notion. It became more acceptable to live with lovers than marry, and divorce became an easy solution to unwanted marriage with the judiciary making allowances that its predecessors refused. Contraceptives, abortions and planned parenthood have severely decreased the European birthrate while other ethnicities spread among the Caucasian populations of Europe and America and continued to fill hospitals with infants. Dogs and cats, long ago regarded as guardians of property and the home from rodents and wild animals are, to Ursula's amazement, now made into pets as mankind becomes fat and gluttonous. Ursula lived during a time when animals were either food or tools, and indolence and obesity were considered sin or the vice of royalty.

Now in lines 72-75 her prophecies take on a noticeable change. For the first and *only* time in her poem does she provide an actual year-date. . . 1926. Second, this is the only time Ursula gives advice rather than descriptions of what she sees. "Build houses light of straw and sticks, for then shall mighty wars be planned, and fire and sword shall sweep the land." Mother Shipton saw the truth about World War II – that it was a premeditated war, planned by globalists and international bankers, and that ". . .half the world, deep drenched in blood shall die [line 79]." Even now it can only be found in specialist literature that *hundreds of millions* of people during World War II died, mostly *after* the war was concluded, as huge populations of civilians in Germany vanished, taken by the Russians. Millions of Russians vanished; many millions in eastern block nations were also exterminated in programs in China and Southeast Asia. The western media giants totally ignored these foreign military programs. The Great War was planned and financed as early as 1926 but Mother Shipton provides the timing through her poem – "*When* pictures seem alive with movements free; *When* boats like fishes swim in the sea; *When* men like birds shall scour the sky; *Then* half the world, deep-drenched in blood shall die." The 1930s and 40s saw the wide scale international emergence of all of these things – movies, submarines and aircraft.

Line 80 begins our serious study. Mother Shipton had just described in the previous line *a global depopulation* of catastrophic proportions that began in the 1940s and now Ursula moves through future history to the *next* great global depopulation of the world in 2040 AD in line 80:

"For those who live the *century through* . . ."

2040 is 100 years after 1940. Just as death and destruction were carried out through 1941-1946, even a year after the conclusion of the Great War, so too will ruin, death, violence, plague and chaos continue in 2041, 2042, 2043, 2044, 2045 and of course in 2046. Ursula Southeil, daughter of an English witch, who was born in 1488, the year planet Phoenix silently passed through the inner solar system, now describes what she sees in 2040 AD.

people will fear and tremble [lines 81, 90]

flee to the mountains and dens [lines 82-83]

suffer storms, tumultuous oceans [84]

see doom approaching for *seven days* [92-93]

oceans pass over land [94-95]

earthquakes break the world [96-97]

violence between men [101-105, 107-109]

scarcity of food [103]

flooding habitations [106]

disaster ending, humanity survives [110-113]

This is the first global cataclysm described by Mother Shipton. She wrote that ". . .old worlds die and new be born." [line 87] She has provided an accurate description of what occurred in 2239 BC when Phoenix appeared for *seven days* before the Great Flood, what those survivors of the Archaic Civilization experienced in 1687 BC, then again in the Middle Bronze Age in 1135 BC. She calls the cause of this almost-total destruction of the world a "fiery dragon," which mirrors the early historical descriptions of comets and celestial bodies mentioned in the oldest records of the east. Sky Dragons were terrible sights appearing in the heavens that wrought ruin upon the world. Her description of it as being the *sixth* visitation of the sky dragon serves to remind us that this is the *Sixth* Seal of the Apocalypse in Revelation 6:12-17, which concerns the 2040 AD Phoenix transit.

great earthquake [verse 12]

sun darkened [verse 12]

moon red as blood [verse 12]

meteoric rain [verse 13]

pole shift, crustal slippage [verse 14]

islands, mountains moved [verse 14]

men terrified [verse 15]

men hide in dens and mountains [verse 15]

This is merely the Revelation account. If one includes all of the other Old Testament, New Testament and apocryphal prophetic passages [as does *When the Sun Darkens*] then a much more complete picture of the cataclysm develops. Mother Shipton's birth in 1488 was 138 years before Phoenix would enter the inner system again in 1626. Though again unseen because it did not transit, in this same year New Amsterdam was founded, which would later be renamed New *York*. Counting another 138 years of orbital time, we arrive at 1764 when astronomer Hoffman was amazed to see a gigantic planetary body pass over one-fifth of the surface of the sun traveling on a north-to-south orbit – unlike any other known planet in the solar system. It was also seen by people all over Europe with the naked eye. In 1764 the orbits of Earth and Phoenix began realigning as they had always done anciently, just before terrible global catastrophes. Phoenix returned in 1902 when the first skyscraper was built – the Fuller Building in New York City. At 21 stories, it is a one-of-a-kind edifice shaped like a giant cheese wedge. It is an official New York landmark. Also in 1902 meteorologists from around the world reported strange cosmic phenomena. Dust, dirt and mud rained in the hundreds of millions of tons over the earth, even from clear blue skies. Fragments of large objects passing the earth in 1902 and 1903 cast their shadows upon whole cities and regions. And of course, 138 years later it will be 2040.

That Mother Shipton wrote about the Phoenix cataclysm is irrefutable. But she did more than that. Like Nostradamus, the Northern Prophetess saw beyond to a much *more* destructive and horrible event. She wrote:

> And when the dragon's tail is gone,
> Man forgets, and smiles, and carries on,
> To apply himself-too late too late,
> For mankind has earned deserved fate. [lines 110-113]

> His masked smile-his false grandeur,
> Will serve the Gods their anger stir,
> And they will send the Dragon back
> To light the sky-his tail will crack,
> Upon the earth and rend the earth
> And man shall flee, king, lord and serf. [114-119]

By the context of her predictions she dated the first cataclysmic episode at 2040, the second being shortly after. This is NIBIRU, the Anunnaki homeworld. This is supported by the chronology of the Book of Revelation. As Phoenix causes the Sixth Seal events, NIBIRU is the celestial cause of the *Trumpet* judgments that follow the breaking of the Seven Seals. Here are the particulars of Ursula's *second* cataclysm:

> dragon lights the sky [line 117]
> dragon's tail strikes the earth [117-118]
> earth is broken [118]
> kings and serfs shall flee [119]
> drought and thirst [lines 121-122]
> oceans pass over coasts [123]
> earthquakes, lands split [124]
> humans live on ocean beds [133, 140-143]
> many lands sink under ocean [136]
> landmasses covered with rotting corpses
> [137-138]
> lands rise out of the sea [140-141]

The last time NIBIRU passed through the inner system was in 1314 AD after orbiting the sun for 60 years before traveling back out into the Kuiper Belt for another 732 years, until its 2046 return. Its total orbit is fixed at 792 years. In 1314 it appeared as a great black darkness that blocked out the stars and the east was afflicted with meteoric rain, quakes and flooding. NIBIRU will push our world into a tighter orbit around the sun effectively abbreviating the solar year from 365.25 days to 240 days. Earth, closer to the sun, will rotate faster, shortening the length of day and night. All of this is fully explained in *Anunnaki Homeworld*. NIBIRU is seen clearly in the Revelation record and its effect and appearance is found in Rev. chapter 8: the first four Trumpets.

> fire from heaven to earth [verse 8:5]
> thunderings, lightning, quake [8:5]
> hail and fire mingled with blood [8:7]
> a third of trees and vegetation burned [8:7]
> gigantic meteorite into sea [8:8]
> a third of sea becomes contaminated [8:8]
> a third of sea life dies [8:9]
> a third of ships sink [8:9]
> great star from heaven [8:10]

great star contaminates third of fresh water
[8:10-11]
great star named Wormwood [8:10-11]
a third of sun, moon, stars smitten [8:12]
a third of day and night reduced [8:12]

Wormwood has always been a source of mystery; it is the star that does not impact. It is NIBIRU. Ursula describes the source of contamination perfectly, that earth *passes through* the tail of the dragon. Looking back to the date-index of the prophet Nostradamus we now recall what he said for the year 2046. Century 2/quatrain 46 reads:

> *Following one great human tragedy*, a great-
> er lies in wait. The mighty movement of the
> centuries begins renewal. Rain, Blood, milk,
> famine, sword and the plague. Fire will be
> seen in the sky, with a trail of sparks.

The Yorkshire Prophecy of Mother Shipton was first popularized from what we know in the year 1740 in Tyrrel's book. So from her birth in 1488 to the publication of her prophecies in 1740 was *252 years,* a time when books were being distributed all over England and Europe due to the popular usage of the printing press. Mother Shipton's prophecies, published for the first time in 1740, serves us as an isometric epicentral year. Counting this same *252 years* we arrive at the date of 1992, when Mother Shipton's Yorkshire Prophecy was publicized again and published in *Nexus* magazine, Volume 2, No.3. The author is also indebted to David Hatcher Childress for immortalizing this amazing prophecy in the pages of his book, *A Hitchhiker's Guide to Armageddon.*

But this isometric projection is but a drop in the bucket compared to those we will now review.

V

Isometric Projections of 2040 AD

It would be a miracle indeed, if all these coincidences were purely accidental. Anyone familiar with the theory of probabilities knows that with every additional coincidence the chances for another grow smaller.
—Immanuel Velikovsky (1)

If we could view the history of the world from a geometrical position outside of its events we would see from this unique vantage point wave-rings of events moving backward and forward in time without impeding one another. The trillions of concentric rings ever spanning outward flow through one another effortlessly and the interference subtly alters a conceptual present from its ancestral past.

People are racially and spatially connected to their ancestors and their descendants, the events experienced now forging the future patterns just as the present has been constructed from a multitude of pasts. It is a seemingly infinite matrix of disconnected events that begin at many different times and converge in the here and now to build the present. We are, essentially, descendants of history, as historical events were themselves conceived from those that preceded them.

If the present is forged out of patterns whose geometrical reflections turned space into solids out of fleeting present reality, then the phenomenon of time, which is merely the motion and change of position of physical objects, should be measured in patterns that reflect this truth. Immersed in this material existence, which is governed by the motion of its own dimensions, we cannot help but instinctively know that all space and time is measured and that by our perception of past and present events, we can know the future.

By studying present and past events we can fathom a future. This is the study of calendrical isometrics. Isometric projections can be a method by which to:

1. determine the beginning or end of a specific timeline;

2. demonstrate that prediction and prophecy can have an scientific explanation;

3. observe retrospectively that events (phenomena) are fixed in the collective although individually we have the power to determine our own position (relation) to the events.

The third is a challenging statement and since men began to ponder these mysteries there have been many among the learned who have been offended at this concept. This does not refer to free will or the choices we make; only to events in a broader, foundational sense. That the future is predetermined is easily discovered when regarding an accurate past, especially when reviewing the patterns of cataclysmic astronomical cycles. But *pre-destination* only applies to the geometry of *our spatial conditions*, which form the parameters of our existence. For example, we have great latitude in deciding for ourselves who we want to be, who we are, what we do, what we want to do, where we go and where we want to go, and *when* we want these things within this space-time structure. We are not puppets, but *images* of something else and we *flow through events*, traveling through the fixed geometry of what we call reality, ever deciding for ourselves the conditions which we subject ourselves to.

Free will defines us as travelers *within* a fixed and unchangeable geometry. We are the reason the geometry exists and our destiny is to exit this space-time structure so we can enter the next. Where that is located depends on one's trajectory within the present construction and is a matter between each of the created and the Creator.

And because human institutions and civilizations had a beginning point within the fixed dimensions of history, they were given a definite end. Our duty, responsibility and goal is to see beyond the structures that presently confine us, so we can more accurately see where we are going.

The pool is not a sea of endless water. It has boundaries. Ripples in the pond of time traverse one another until they make contact with these immovable boundaries. The waves slightly change form and reflect back, flowing through other ripples and the interference patterns result with slight modifications of the events, but do not alter them into something else. For example, in a hologram a lizard is a lizard and nothing else, albeit there may be 10,000 variations within the species. In this pool the tadpole and minnow swim through the infinite patterns of events *unknowingly*. Breaking the surface, poking their heads out into the open air, they sometimes create interference patterns of their own but the parameters of the pool can never change by any conscious or unconscious acts of the tadpole or minnow. The boundaries are fixed.

We defer to the erudition of Professor Soddy who in 1911 said, "Civilization, as it is at present, even on a purely physical side, is not a continuous self-supporting movement. The conditions under which it originates determine *its period* and *fix the date* of its decline."

Our first glimpse of calendrical isometrics concerned the World Trade Center destruction in New York. Now we will peer deeper into the history of the world in our search of what to expect in 2040.

The first example is evidently the simplest because it involves the astronomical period of Phoenix. In 1902 Phoenix blanketed the earth in dust and mud, sometimes as much as 50 tons per square mile.(2) A volcano named Mt. Pelee exploded on the French Caribbean island of Martinique, incinerating 30,000 people in an instant in May, and another volcano in Santa Maria, Guatemala, killed 1000 people. In the United States in 1902 the U.S. Census Bureau was founded. Washington, DC was planned out with the Capitol reworked to employ geometrical arrangements through its streets and districts. In New York City the first skyscraper was built, the Fuller Building. This particular year, 1902, is an isometric epicenter, being *138 years* after 1764 AD when Phoenix was visually seen to pass over one-fifth of the sun's surface by the naked eye and by a European astronomer through a telescope. Counting this same *138 years* after 1902 is 2040.

> *Isometric Projection Interpretation*: In 2040 planet Phoenix will be visually seen, earth will be bathed in cosmic dust clouding up the atmosphere in May, volcanic activity will result in high fatalities in the mid-Atlantic ocean, architecture of New York and Washington DC will come to an end with loss of American population [census].

In 1980 on May 18-19 the long-dormant volcano, Mount St. Helens, exploded causing widespread environmental ruin in the western United States. This massive explosion resulted with few fatalities because of the mountain's rural location. Also in 1980 an earthquake in southern Italy killed 3000 people, and amazingly, at Peekskill, *New York* a red Chevrolet Malibu was struck by a *meteorite* the size of a football that penetrated the entire vehicle, passed through the gas tank and impacted the concrete, forming a crater six inches deep.(3) This was *60.5 years* after 1919, when Mount Kelud in Indonesia erupted killing 5000 people in *May*. Counting *60.5 years* after 1980 is 2040.

> *Isometric Projection Interpretation*: In 2040
> volcanic activity in the western United States
> and in the Far East, both bordering the Pa-
> cific, will result in wide-scale ecological ruin.
> Southern Europe will experience seismic ac-
> tivity in May, both the volcanoes and quakes
> will have high death tolls.

In 1965 a comet is seen. A windstorm afflicts Bangladesh, India killing 17,000 people in *May*, followed by a second windstorm that killed 30,000 and a third storm in December that killed 10,000 more. In the northeastern United States the Great Blackout occurred, darkening *New York* and surrounding regions. Power companies not even connected to the main power grid went offline and VLF frequency and Ham radio reception were jammed with static, all indicating not a power outage, but a powerful electromagnetic disturbance. (4) This was *75 years* after 1890, when hail with sandstone pebbles rained from the skies of France in June, and previously in *May* a substance like blood rained upon Messignai, Calabria. It was sent to Rome for analysis and to everyone's amazement it was discovered to be *real blood*.(5) In October of the same year people looked up to see a comet-like object pass across 100 degrees of the sky at an incredible velocity in 45 minutes from Grahamstown. (6) Counting *75 years* after 1965 in 2040.

> *Isometric Projection Interpretation*: India
> suffers a massive loss of population due to
> repeated storms in 2040, these are connected
> to electromagnetic interference and stress
> between a celestial body approaching earth.
> Recall that Nostradamus in his 2040 AD qua-

> trains mentioned back-to-back *storms*. New
> York will lose electricity as will most of the
> northeastern seaboard. Telecommunications
> will be ineffective and hail, sand and rocks
> will rain from the skies and blood will rain
> on earth in May. Nostradamus too refers to
> blood from the skies. This indicates that fro-
> zen landscapes fragmenting off a shattered
> planet will enter the atmosphere containing
> the organic remains of ancient life forms
> that lived long ago, before their world was
> destroyed and frozen. People will behold one
> or more gigantic objects passing close to the
> earth.

In 1886 the Statue of Liberty, made in France, was sent to New York. Also in this year astronomers reported seeing a large moonlike object in the inner solar system near Venus. This was *154 years* after 1732, when people watched fiery globes cross the sky over Swabia, which preceded an earthquake on May 28th.(7) Counting *154 years* after 1886 is 2040.

> *Isometric Projection Interpretation*: The
> landmark monument, the Statue of Liberty,
> is destroyed. A large celestial body enters the
> inner solar system and strange things are seen
> burning in the upper atmosphere moments
> before earthquakes occur.

The year 1890, as we just reviewed, was visited with hail and pebbles raining on France in June and blood falling from the skies in May with a comet-like object in October passing 100 degrees of the sky at an incredible velocity. But 1890 is also an isometric epicenter for a different projection involving 2040. It was *150 years* after 1740 when telescope maker and astronomer James Short discovered a planet-sized object passing through the inner solar system near Venus. Also in 1740 the predictions of Mother Shipton were published widely for the first time in Tyrrel's *The Yorkshire Prophecy*. Counting *150 years* after 1890 is 2040.

> *Isometric Projection Interpretation*: A large
> celestial body will enter the inner solar sys-

tem in 2040 bringing hail, rocks and blood to
fall upon the earth, *fulfilling* the predictions
of the Northern Prophetess concerning the
destruction of earth by the Sky Dragon.

In 1862 black spots were reported to be passing and a comet appeared
having a very nebulous tail. This was *178* years after 1684 when astronomers
reported the appearance of a comet in May.(8) Counting *178* years after 1862
is 2040.

Isometric Projection Interpretation: In 2040
a comet-like object will enter the inner solar system with a spectacular tail. In May a
strewn field of asteroids and glacial masses
pass between earth and the sun.

In 1846 a comet named Biela was seen to have fragmented by astronomers.
Another comet appears and is named Bronson, with astronomers asserting
that it does not orbit the sun, but some other *unknown body*.(9) In this same
year astronomers discover planet Neptune at the outer edge of the solar
system, initially found by German astronomer Galle. This was *194 years* after
1652 when astronomers in Europe reported the appearance of a new comet in
November(10), after a burning meteorite crashed between Siena and Rome in
May.(11) Counting *194 years* after 1846 is 2040.

Isometric Projection Interpretation: Comets
enter the inner solar system but orbit a gigantic planetary body that is reported by astronomers at the edge of the solar system. Planet
Phoenix is seen and Italy or southern Europe
suffers meteoric rain in May. Readers of
When the Sun Darkens will recall that when
Phoenix passed through the inner system in
1902, it brought with it a formerly unknown
comet that was named Morehouse.

In 1908 a bright flash illuminated the sky over Asia and a comet-like body
exploded in the air above Tunguska, Siberia. The blast splintered forests for
hundreds of miles like matchsticks and knocked people off their feet even a
hundred miles away. The pressure of the blast affected barometers in England

and sunsets for weeks were spectacular due to *cosmic dust*. This occurred in June. Later in the year an earthquake at Messina, Sicily, was followed by a tsunami that killed 120,000 people.(12) On July 2 over Braemar, thunder was heard high in the sky on a clear day with the sun shining, followed by pieces of ice that fell from the sky.(13) This was *132 years* after 1776 when the North American 13 Colonies declared their independence from England, the beginning of the mighty United States of America. In *May* of 1776 an order of globalists was founded called the *Illuminati*, agents of foreign powers that sought to control and destroy the free republics and democracies emerging throughout Europe and North America. Counting *132 years* after 1908 is 2040.

> *Isometric Projection Interpretation*: In 2040 the areas of Asia will suffer cosmic impacts and atmospheric detonations of extraterrestrial materials, as cosmic dust and debris envelope earth. The Mediterranean Sea suffers seismic activity that causes tidal waves to destroy entire cities with massive loss of life. Glacial fragments enter the atmosphere and rain in pieces. The enemies of the United States will exult over the ruin of the once-mighty empire.

In 1808 many people in North America watched in stunned fascination as a long procession of meteors passed overhead for *two hours* on May 16th. Some were seen to fall to earth and when the areas were searched the people discovered a strange gelatinous substance on the ground.(14) This was *231.5 years* after 1577 when a bright comet was viewed from Europe and North America. In December, many black objects passing through the sky were seen from Wittenberg, Germany.(15) Counting *231.5 years* after May of 1808 is 2040.

> *Isometric Projection Interpretation*: In 2040 celestial objects in space will be viewed from the Northern Hemisphere in May, which supports the fact that Phoenix, on its descending node from north of the ecliptic, would be best seen north of the equator.

In 1202 AD at the height of a famine in Egypt that had already caused widespread starvation, a series of earthquakes began on May 20th. Ships out at harbor in the Mediterranean were *pulled away* from the coast and never seen again.(16) This was *837.5 years* after 365 AD when, in July, an earthquake shook Alexandria and northern Egypt. Roman historian Ammianus Marcellinus wrote that the quake was preceded by lightning and thunder in the sky that continued through the quaking. The Mediterranean coast *withdrew* as the sea disappeared northward, exposing the seabed to the air. Thousands of people ran out picking up fish and shells but a sudden tidal wave returned, overtaking these unfortunate people. The tsunami flooded Alexandria and even deposited ships atop buildings. When the water receded many more people were pulled out to sea to die. About 50,000 people lost their lives.(17) Marcellinus wrote that the disaster affected the whole Mediterranean world, Aegean islands and coasts where whole ships and their dead crews could be found near Mothone in the Pelopponesus.(18) Counting *837.5 years* after May of 1202 is 2040.

> *Isometric Projection Interpretation*: In 2040
> terrible seismic activity in the Mediterranean
> world will destroy islands and coastal cit-
> ies, as the Mediterranean Sea overextends its
> boundaries to the ruin of property and lives
> north and south of the basin.

In 1914 a typhus epidemic killed millions of people from Europe to Russia. World War I began, involving both European powers and Russia and on the first day of the First Battle of Somme, the British suffered 57,470 casualties against the Germans, 19,240 of them being men killed in combat. The Japanese volcano Sakurjima erupted burying many buildings. This was *126 years* after 1788 when the astronomer Schroeter witnessed lights appearing on the surface of the moon in the lunar mountains. When sunlight touched that same region there was a shadow cast where the lights had been seen, which indicated that these lights were lunar *volcanoes*.(19) In New York the first Federal Congress was held. Counting *126 years* after 1914 is 2040.

> *Isometric Projection Interpretation*: In 2040
> a world war will erupt in the northern hemi-
> sphere of Eurasia as well as a tragic epidemic
> as volcanic activity occurs in the Pacific. Vol-
> canic activity will occur on the moon as well.

The *final* time Congress will meet in New
York is in this year.

In 1853 the city of New York hosted the first World's Fair held in the
United States. Remember, it was the first World's Fair ever that was hosted
in England inside the Crystal Palace, predicted by Mother Shipton. This was
187 years after 1666 AD, the infamous year when the Great Fire of London
destroyed the city. London was the *New York* of Europe. Incidentally, as is so
commonly shown in many of books on Nostradamus, the fiery destruction of
London was predicted by the French seer. Counting *187 years* after 1853 is
2040.

> *Isometric Projection Interpretation*: New
> York City is destroyed and ceases to be the
> frontline of global industry, economics (Wall
> Street) and politics (United Nations base).
> London in southern Britain is also destroyed,
> just as Nostradamus infers in his quatrains.

In 1880 the ancient Egyptian obelisk of Thutmose is set up in Central
Park, New York – a monument originally quarried, moved and erected by
the Israelites subservient to Pharaoh in 1515 BC. Also in 1880 a series of
genocidal programs in Russia prompted millions of people to migrate, the
majority Jews fleeing the persecution, with hundreds of thousands escaping
across the Atlantic to enter the United States through the immigration offices
of *New York City*. This is *160 years* after 1720, when people in New York and
throughout the Northern Hemisphere observed a bright comet, named Nexel.
Counting *160 years* after 1880 is 2040.

> *Isometric Projection Interpretation*: The
> Obelisk in Central Park will be toppled, a
> monument that will then be 3,554 years old.
> Great masses of people will flee New York
> and a new celestial body will be clearly seen
> in the heavens.

In 1916 over a million casualties were documented in the Second Battle of
Somme during World War I between France and Germany. But those soldiers
lost in this one battle were only a fraction of the total death toll France suffered
during this tragic war. This was *124 years* after 1792, the year of the founding
of the *French* Revolution. Counting *124 years* after 1916 is 2040.

> *Isometric Projection Interpretation*: In 2040
> will come an end to the French government
> and millions of French people will die.

In 1915 Professor Barnard studied the strange region in space around the constellation Cephus in the northern circumpolar sphere. At that location in space he discovered a vast blackness – an object near the star Algol [the Ghoul], which was considered by the ancients to be the most evil of all stars. This was *125 years* after 1790 when the Spanish excavated the mysterious Aztec Stone of the Fifth Sun, which depicts the Four Ages of the Sun, or Phoenix transits, and predicts the Fifth Sun dying (return of Phoenix). The relic, known also as the Aztec Calendar Stone, is a virtual Mesoamerican version of the Apocalypse. Counting *125 years* after 1915 is 2040.

> *Isometric Projection Interpretation*: A celes-
> tial object will descend out of the northern
> circumpolar region of space, north of the
> ecliptic, and bring with it the anciently under-
> stood and predicted Apocalypse.

Professor Barnard was an avid astronomer. His 1915 discovery was not his first glimpse of the heavens relative to this book. Twenty-three years earlier in 1892 Barnard, using a 36-inch Lick Refractor telescope, discovered a *planet beyond Neptune* that could not have been Pluto, as Pluto is so small that even the Hubble space telescope can only return blurred images of it. The scientific community met his astonishing discovery with silence and the discovery was not made known to the public until the 1906 August edition of *Nature*.(20) He got a one-time glimpse of Phoenix, approaching exactly 10 years before it would pass through the inner system in its descending node out of the northern sky. Astronomers could not verify Barnard's discovery because of their obstinate position that a planet had to be located along the *ecliptic plane*, refusing that planetary-sized objects could mimic cometary orbits. Also in 1892 in *April*, the Dutch astronomer Muller watched dark objects float between earth and the moon.(21) Remarkably, in *The Complete Story of the San Francisco Horror* published in 1906 we find (on page 234) that in April of 1892 a severe earthquake rocked San Francisco, followed by another two days later. This was *148 years* after 1744 when the entire Northern Hemisphere populations from North America to Europe were terrified by the appearance of the Great Daytime Comet, which had seven tails and caused much apocalyptic fever.(22) Astronomers named it comet De Cheseaux. Counting *148 years* after 1892 is 2040.

> *Isometric Projection Interpretation*: In 2040,
> early in the year, professional and probably
> amateur astronomers will view planet Phoe-
> nix at the edge of the solar system far above
> the ecliptic and report their findings to vari-
> ous agencies and world governments. These
> reports will be *ignored* and the private sector
> will not be notified. The object will come into
> view and terrify the inhabitants of the world
> (recall that by all ancient and prophetic ac-
> counts, Phoenix appears for seven days).

In 1968 astronomers at Harvard University at their observatory discovered a large asteroid, and trajectoral analysis determined that it was on a collision course with Earth. The asteroid was several miles across and if impact occurred it would be globally catastrophic. The object had initially been seen in 1967 but the astronomers predicted impact in 1968, during the month of June. The discovery was made known to government officials but never brought to the public's attention. It was watched carefully and missed the earth by only a million miles(23), this being a very short distance in astronomical space. The sun is 93 million miles away. This was *36 years before* 2004 when astronomers discovered another near-earth asteroid, naming it Apophis. Counting *36 years* after 2004 is 2040.

> *Isometric Projection Interpretation*: In 2040
> a large object will be seen approaching the
> earth. Though it will be reported to the au-
> thorities, the authorities will not relay the
> information to the public.

On June 15, 1896 a submarine earthquake in the Tuscarora Deep, south of Japan, caused the Pacific sea to recede, leaving behind drying ocean bed with stranded sea creatures. Multitudes of Japanese went out and gathered the animals up for food but were overtaken as a 90 foot high wave returned at 450 miles-per-hour and slammed into the coast, flooding far inland and washing whole villages out to sea. Over 30,000 people were lost at sea and died. This disaster very closely mirrors what happened to Alexandria, Egypt in 365 AD. Also in 1896, A.P. Sinnett in *The Growth of the Soul* wrote that there exists *two more planets* in our solar system *beyond Neptune*.(24) This would be Phoenix and NIBIRU. This was *144 years* after 1752, when on April 15 over

Norway (facing circumpolar heavens) the people witnessed a strange, star-like object of octagonal shape pass across the sky, and over Augermannland were seen balls of fire streaking across the sky.(25) Counting *144 years* after 1896 is 2040.

> *Isometric Projection Interpretation*: In 2040
> seismic activity in the Pacific will result
> in tidal waves and widespread loss of life
> among Asian people. Though the billions liv-
> ing on earth before the cataclysm are largely
> unaware of the approaching doom, there will
> *be many who are informed*, people who read
> about or were told that this global catastrophe
> was coming. The sky will show a stunning
> celestial object unlike any seen in modern
> history, appearing in the northern heavens.

In 1811 the New Madrid Earthquakes rocked the eastern United States in a series of the most widespread and powerful quakes on record. The quakes were experienced from New York to Florida, causing church bells to toll in Virginia as bell towers were shook. Centered in Missouri, the quakes happened in late 1811 after the appearance of the Great Comet. At one point the Mississippi River was observed to flow backward and in Kentucky the renowned naturalist John James Audubon, among others, heard a roaring in the sky and thought it was a tornado. They observed a *darkening of the sky*, albeit unusual, that later brightened back to normal.(26) This was *229 years* after 1582 when a comet appeared and brought a terrible plague upon Thuringia and the Netherlands.(27) Counting *229 years* after 1811 is 2040.

> *Isometric Projection Interpretation*: Dur-
> ing a darkening of the sky in 2040, terrible
> earthquakes will occur from Missouri to New
> York, Virginia and Florida, and the coastal
> regions of the North Atlantic. An object ap-
> proaching earth will be seen by Europeans
> and a deadly epidemic will begin.

It would seem that when isometric projections span several centuries, their likelihood should become less probable since, with the extension of time between events, there would be found fewer and fewer parallels. But this is not the case. The reason is because time and events are *positioned* within a three-dimensional structure; a fourth dimension can never be static because everything continues to move. Isometric projections demonstrate the *fixed* geometrical parameters of this 4th-dimensional universe that we, as individuals, *flow* through, in a backdrop of multitudes of pasts.

In 1797 at Quito, Ecuador an earthquake killed 41,000 people. This was *243 years* after 1554 AD when the prophecies of Nostradamus were finished and edited by the secretary of the French seer named Jean-Aymes De Chavigny. (28) Of course, these *Centuries* predicted and dated the 2040 AD cataclysm and encoded the name Phoenix as well as its 138-year orbit. Counting *243 years* after 1797 is 2040.

> *Isometric Projection Interpretation*: Seismic activity in the Central American and North-South American regions will result in high death tolls. Planet Phoenix will cause global destruction, fulfilling many prophecies.

In 1677 Europeans witnessed a comet appearance in April.(29) This was *363 years* after 1314 AD, when planet NIBIRU passed through the inner system and darkened the sun over Asia causing storms, meteoric rain, quakes, flooding and plague-fogs. Europe gazed in horror at the night sky, as a great blackness darkened the stars. This event is well documented in *Anunnaki Homeworld*. Counting *363 years* after 1677 is 2040.

> *Isometric Projection Interpretation*: This unique pattern has NIBIRU at the far past and Phoenix at the future end of the projection, with the appearance of the comet as the isometric epicenter. Obviously, in 2040 AD, a hitherto scientifically unrecognized intruder planet will approach the inner system, pass close to earth and be the cause of worldwide geological changes and epic disasters.

In 1303 AD during a short period known to historians as the Seven Comets over Europe (1298-1314 AD), an earthquake afflicted Egypt, some believing that it toppled the remains of the famous Pharos Lighthouse.(30) This was *737 years* after 566 AD, when brilliant lights appeared in the skies and, according to Gregory of Tours, the heavens appeared to be on fire.(31) Counting *737 years* after 1303 is 2040.

> *Isometric Projection Interpretation*: In 2040
> AD, just after a period of heightened comet
> activity, an earthquake will rock the southern
> Mediterranean and Egypt, as objects entering
> the upper atmosphere brighten the skies over
> Europe.

In 1290 an earthquake at Chihli, China killed 100,000 people.(32) This was *750 years* after 540 AD when a *total eclipse of the sun occurred* that did not involve the moon. Something else transited between earth and the sun, casting at least the British Isles in shadow. This is recorded in the Anglo-Saxon Chronicle. Also in 540 the bubonic plague, killing thousands daily, overspread from the east and spilled into Roman provincial territories and the Roman domains of Justinian. Counting *750 years* after 1290 is 2040.

> *Isometric Projection Interpretation*: In 2040
> a celestial body will pass between the earth
> and the sun and cast the world in shadows as
> earthquakes and plague kill countless multi-
> tudes in the east. Ruin, disease and death will
> spread across the world from the east toward
> the west.

Our final example of isometric patterns involving 2040 concerns again the year 1902, the last time Phoenix passed through the inner system on its 138-year orbital journey before returning in 2040. The year 1971 is our calendrical epicenter, being *69 years* after 1902 and 69 years before 2040. In 1971 the CIA was deeply entrenched in the jungles of Southeast Asia during the Vietnam War in an intelligence operation referred to by the Vietnamese as Phuong-Hoang – but the U.S. government called it Project *Phoenix*. This operation was a joint effort between Vietnamese and Americans and the intelligence gathered resulted in the deaths of untold thousands.(33) The critic will hurry and call this coincidence, but the astute student of history, seeing through the lens of isometric projections, will know that coincidences are merely the reemergence of past space-time reflections.

We conclude this chapter on 2040 with a quote from Thomas Troward, from the year 1902:

A relation once clearly grasped in its mathematical aspect becomes thenceforth one
of the unalterable truths of the universe. No
longer a thing to be argued about, but an
axiom that may be assumed as the foundation
on which to build up the edifice of further
knowledge.(34)

VI

Isometric Projections of 2046 AD

The past that is already dead remains present
in the future that has yet to be born.
—Lewis Mumford, *Technics and Civilization*

The events of the year 2046 are not dissimilar from those of 2040. Both are globally destructive, both result in at least a billion deaths and both are caused by intruder planets known and feared by the ancients. Some of the historic disasters cited in the previous chapter and linked isometrically to 2040 reappear in isometric projections connected to 2046, howbeit, they are themselves connected to other, as yet undisclosed events. 2046 has many of its own calendrical surprises.

Both Ursula Southeil and Nostradamus focused on the first cataclysm, dating it at 2040. Both mentioned the second catastrophe but neither really concentrated on it and both declared that the second was to be worse than the first. Naturally, one would think that they would have focused their attention on the second cataclysm, but this is not the case. There is an explanation for this.

The world as we know and have built it will end in 2040. The comforts and innovations of this electricity-dependent civilization will end – no more artificial lightning supported by power grids, air conditioning, heating, microwaves, refrigerated foods. Whole cities, states and nations will be reduced to rubble. Industry, manufacturing and commerce will cease. The convenience of grocery stores and restaurants will be a memory. Starvation will induce people to do horrible things and without operable hospitals, disease and plague will run rampant. There will be no inoculations and infant mortality will be severe. With a major pole shift, the geography of the world will be altered, the seas too chaotic to traverse and airports and aircraft virtually non-existent.

Men will be catapulted into positions of social superiority as Bronze Age culture returns, our world plummeting into those cultural institutions prominent during the Early and Late Bronze Age, when planet Phoenix darkened the sun and caused global ruin in 2239 BC, 1687 BC and 1135 BC. Women, having enjoyed unprecedented rights, privileges and immunities from the days of suffrage until now in social, corporate and marital status or independence will find themselves willingly offering their bodies for protection, food and shelter. Those resisting will be brutalized, owned, enslaved and used for barter. Gangland dictatorships will carve their kingdoms out of the lands as murder-for-sport, pedophilia and cannibalism become societal norms. Bands of survivors trying to rebuild communities will have to protect themselves from roving gangs and militant orders that seek to take what they have. Haunted people in mass migrations will wander the earth in no particular direction, searching for sustenance.

After all this begins there is really no reason for Mother Shipton or Nostradamus to elaborate further on the second and far worse disaster. It would be redundant. The second cataclysm can not possibly do more damage than the first, which virtually ends 500 years of techno-industrial civilization. It is described by both of them as worse because it will result in a higher *death toll*. Phoenix, as the Sixth Seal of the Apocalypse, will cause a *fourth* of the world's population to perish, but NIBIRU, referred to as Wormwood in the Bible's Revelation, initiates the Trumpet judgments that result in the death of a *third* of mankind. This is not a third of the people living on earth in total, but a third of those surviving after Phoenix kills 25% of humanity. Thus, about 50% of mankind will die between both of these horrific events – the second killing more than the first, but the first ending our *way of life* altogether.

Let us now review the Isometric Projections involving 2046 AD.

In 1918, throughout Europe and Asia, an epidemic killed 20,000,000 people at the end of World War I, which in itself resulted in millions of casualties. This was *128 years* after the 1790 discovery of the Aztec Stone of the Fifth Sun. This apocalypse in stone not only pictographically refers to the Phoenix disaster in 2040, but also specifically refers to the 2046 AD cataclysm when Earth will be *moved out of its place*. The Aztec relic depicts the "day of 4-Movement" as a pyramid with crossed bars and an "eye" above it. This day, 4-Movement, marks the time in the future when a terrible disaster will occur. The crossed bars are a symbol from older Mesoamerican cultures that refer to the passage of an age, a period of time. Incredibly, this image on the Aztec artifact reflects what David Davidson discovered in 1924 in the geometry of the Great Pyramid's base diagonals (crossed bars) that provided him with the date of 2045 for the termination of an Astronomical Chronology encoded within the Great Pyramid, as explained in *Anunnaki Homeworld*. Also in this book is shown conclusive proof that the Mayan Long-Count calendar was never intended to end in 2012, but the 13-baktun count timeline ends precisely in *2046 AD*. The Aztec Calendar Stone is full of artistic imagery and archeologists have discovered that five of the animals depicted upon the gigantic relic are not from Mexico proper, but indigenous to the *Mayan* country.(1) The Aztecs, so late in history, merely inherited what had been preserved by the Maya, who in turn inherited their sciences and prophecy from the older Olmeca. Counting *128 years* after 1918 is 2046.

> *Isometric Projection Interpretation*: In 2046 the calendars will be changed because the position of the earth orbiting around the sun will be altered, thus changing the length of the year and length of the days. A new age will begin as an epidemic kills millions and North and Central America are destroyed (Maya origin was North America; relic depicts cataclysmic events). This cataclysm will cause an amazing discovery at the Great Pyramid or within it.

In 1913 people all over North America stared awestruck into the sky as a train of meteors passed 30 miles above in February.(2) This is almost 8000 times closer than our own moon. These objects were witnessed by people in Canada, the United States and in the Atlantic as far south as Bermuda. It began as a luminous body with a tail that grew larger and larger until it was close to the earth and seen to be a whole train of fragments, and they ". . .moved with a peculiar majestic, dignified deliberation. . .it appeared in the distance, and another group emerged from its place of origin. . . ."(3) This was *131.5 years* after 1783 when, through the Revolutionary War, the United States officially won its independence from Great Britain, marking the beginning of the American Empire. Also in 1783 a quake in Calabria, Italy killed 30,000 people. Counting *131.5 years* after 1913 is 2046.

> *Isometric Projection Interpretation*: In 2046 the entire Northern Hemisphere will behold

an amazing astronomical sighting. This will
signal the total end of the United States.
Quakes in the Northern Mediterranean and
Italy will result in high death tolls.

In 1911 flooding kills 100,000 people in China and in this same year the Republic of China is formed. This year is the exact midpoint between the 1776 AD American Independence and the 2046 AD end of the United States, being *135 years* before the Republic of China began. Counting this same *135 years* after 1911 is 2046.

> *Isometric Projection Interpretation*: In 2046
> one superpower finally dies out (USA) as an-
> other is born in the Far East amidst flooding
> and mass fatality. In 2046 the *Kings of the
> East* will become the Superpower, this hav-
> ing been foreseen in biblical prophecies and
> those of Nostradamus.

In 1908 a comet or meteorite exploded in the sky over Tunguska, Siberia as seen in the previous chapter. It destroyed forests for hundreds of miles and knocked people off their feet a hundred miles away. This was *138 years* (Phoenix orbital period) after 1770 when comet Lexell appeared and then passed within 1.39 million miles from the Earth. Counting *138 years* after 1908 is 2046.

> *Isometric Projection Interpretation*: In 2046
> a celestial body will come dangerously close
> to the Earth and debris from this proximity
> will enter our atmosphere and detonate/con-
> taminate.

In 1905 at Kangra, India an earthquake killed 20,000 people. This was *141 years* after 1764 AD when astronomer Hoffman observed through a telescope a gigantic celestial object [Phoenix] passing over one-fifth of the surface of the sun – a sighting also experienced by hundreds of thousands of people in Europe with the naked eye. Counting *141 years* after 1905 is 2046.

> *Isometric Projection Interpretation*: In 2046 a
> huge celestial body will be observed as it ap-

proaches the Earth; quakes will afflict India
resulting in a tragic loss of life.

In 1893 a total eclipse of the sun on November 30th over Santiago, Chili allowed tens of thousands of people a few minutes to gaze up into the darkened sky in amazement to behold a mysterious, reddish and nebulous matter enveloping the earth. After the crimson wisps of clouds in space passed, while the sun was still obscured, a dark object was seen by the people as it passed over the moon.(4) Just prior to this, in October, comet Brooks was *photographed* at the instant it was colliding into some unknown dark object in space, the picture published in the 1894 edition of *Knowledge*.(5) This was *153 years* after 1740 when astronomer James Short discovered a planet-sized object passing through the inner solar system, near Venus.

Isometric Projection Interpretation: In 2046 a
large planetary body will enter the inner solar
system, bathing the earth in cosmic dust, possibly darkening the sun.

In 1883 astronomers reported seeing black objects passing between the earth and sun, irregularly-shaped bodies.(6) An earthquake occurred on the isle of Ishia off Naples and the sea became tumultuous.(7) Earthquakes also happened in Turkey and southern Russia. The ancient volcano on Krakatoa in Indonesia, Mount Anak, exploded with a force equal to 200 twenty-megaton bombs, an explosion so powerful it excavated a hole at the bottom of the Pacific 1900 ft. deep and ejected boulders as far as 25 miles into the atmosphere. The blast sent a tidal wave 100 ft. tall, ruining areas of Java and Sumatra, destroying 300 towns and killing 36,000 people. Volcanic ash left a dust-veil around the entire world for years, darkening the earth and making winters more severe than usual.(8) The explosion was the loudest ever heard by man, heard even 3000 miles away and the quaking was felt around the planet.(9) Scientists have published that it was this dust-veil that cooled the earth and filled the atmosphere with strange sights and, while some of this was true, they concealed from the public that even *before* the volcanic detonation, as early as February, six months earlier, there were many reports of *cosmic dust* blanketing the earth. In November was seen a strange, comet-like object with two tails.(10) This was all *163 years* after 1720, when comet Nexel was seen very brightly and volcanic activity and earthquakes occurred in the Azores. Counting *163 years* after 1883 is 2046.

Isometric Projection Interpretation: A comet-like object will appear in the skies in 2046, attended by volcanic activity and earthquakes in the south Pacific, mid-Atlantic, from Asia Minor (Turkey) to Central Asia and in Russia. Volcanic ash and cosmic dust will fill the atmosphere and the northern Mediterranean Sea will become chaotic as quakes afflict Italy.

In 1859 John Taylor's book *The Great Pyramid: Why Was It Built and Who Built It* was published, becoming an instant sensation in England. It was the first serious attempt to show that the monuments in Egypt were of pre-Flood origin, constructed by patriarchs mentioned in the Bible. In this same year, massive coronal ejections from the sun's surface caused intense electromagnetic storms that reached earth and burned out telegraph wires throughout North America and Europe. Dr. Lescarbault saw black objects passing over the surface of the sun. This was *187 years* after 1672 when European astronomers reported the appearance of a comet.(11) Counting *187 years* after 1859 is 2046.

Isometric Projection Interpretation: A comet-like body will be seen from the Northern Hemisphere that will pass between earth and the sun and cause electromagnetic disruptions of telecommunications technologies. This global event was originally recorded in the Great Pyramid's geometry, an Astronomical Chronology ending in 2046. Recall that the prophet Edgar Cayce referred to the Great Pyramid's importance when the earth will be moved out of its place. Further, as shown in *Anunnaki Homeworld,* the geometrical measurements of the Great Pyramid are a scale model of the *Northern* Hemisphere. It is from the north of the Equator that the Great Pyramid is located – at 30°. The Northern Hemisphere is also the location of what is largely known as the Western Powers, the European, British and Canadian, and United States. . .

those being the nations inferred by the statement earlier made – ". . .the whole western
world will die."

In 1845 comet Biela fragmented into two pieces. This was *200.5 years* after
1645 when astronomers noticed a strange moonlike object near Venus(12) and
the Ming Dynasty of China falls to the Manchus just after a series of natural
disasters, famine and revolts. Counting *200.5 years* after 1845 is 2046.

Isometric Projection Interpretation: In 2046
a large celestial object enters the inner system and appears to be fragmented, as terrible
calamities are already occurring in the Far
East. In this year a new Chinese government
emerges. Recall that this was also found to be
true in the isometric projection involving the
year 1911. This begins the prophetic career
of the Kings of the East. They will begin to
invade the west.

In 1816 Mount Tambora erupted with earthquakes, the detonation heard
over a thousand miles away. An estimated 80,000 people died throughout
Java and Indonesia. Also in 1816, a huge spectacle was seen passing through
the sky that apparently missed the earth.(13) This was *230 years* after 1586
when a volcano killed 10,000 people in *Java and Indonesia*. Counting *230
years* after 1816 is 2046.

Isometric Projection Interpretation: As something appears to approach the earth in space
in 2046, volcanic and seismic activity in Java
and Indonesia will kill tens if not hundreds of
thousands of people.

In 1811 The Great Comet passed through the sky in December and
immediately the greatest earthquake in U.S. history occurred as reviewed in
the prior chapter. Thunder boomed from clear skies, the sky darkened and
the entire eastern seaboard from New York to Florida rocked. This was *234.5
years* after 1577, when astronomers from Altorf, Germany viewed black
objects through their telescopes in the sky in December(14) and a comet
appeared earlier in October.(15) Counting *234.5 years* after 1811 is 2046.

> *Isometric Projection Interpretation*: As objects appear in the sky in 2046, the sky will darken over the northeastern United States and the entire Atlantic coast states will suffer a series of catastrophic earthquakes.

In 1801 G. Piazzi of Palermo, Sicily discovered the asteroid Ceres on January 1st.(16) Astronomers searching for another planet in the empty region between the orbits of Mars and Jupiter, as predicted under the Titius-Bode Law, instead discovered the Asteroid Belt. In this same year, French engineer and archeologist Edme Francois Jomard and astronomer N.A. Nouet counted 203 as the levels of masonry that form the Great Pyramid.(17) This was the first recorded accurate count of the levels of the monument. Once a capstone, or chief cornerstone, is laid atop the structure it will be complete at 204 levels. This was *245 years* after 1556 when in January an earthquake killed 830,000 people in the Shensi Province of China, principally at Shaanxi.(18) Later in April a comet appeared.(19) Counting *245 years* after 1801 is 2046.

> *Isometric Projection Interpretation*: In 2046 astronomers will discover a new celestial member of the solar system and possibly its relation to the Great Pyramid. China will be devastated by seismic activity with a shocking death toll.

In 1759 astronomers reported observing a planet-sized object moving through the inner solar system. Also, Halley's Comet made an appearance and in this year the first scientific exploration of the Great Pyramid was conducted, by Frederick Norden Lewis.(20) This was *287 years* after 1472 when a particularly bright comet appeared and was studied by Johannes Muller, who even made positional calculations for future astronomers.(21) This was also the year Leonardo Da Vinci was born. Counting *287 years* after 1759 is 2046.

> *Isometric Projection Interpretation*: In 2046 a planet-sized body will enter the inner solar system, and perhaps, its relevance to the Great Pyramid will be recognized.

In 1680 a comet appeared in December and was studied by a student of the famous Hevelius named George Dorffel, as well as by John Flamsteed and Edmund Halley.(22) In this year of 1680 the Anunnaki planet NIBIRU was at aphelion, being the furthest distance away from the sun, way out in the Kuiper Belt surrounding our solar system. This was *366 years* after 1314 AD when NIBIRU darkened the sun over Asia causing quakes, floods, volcanic disasters and plagues – but over Europe, which viewed its passing at night, they beheld a black shadow darken the stars and a comet. This year is detailed fully in *Anunnaki Homeworld*. Counting *366 years* after 1680 is 2046.

> *Isometric Projection Interpretation*: In 2046
> planet NIBIRU will pass closely to Earth and
> destroy the Far East, much in the same way
> as planet Phoenix in 2040 destroys the west.

In 1582 a comet appeared and was blamed for a terrible plague that afflicted Thuringia and the Netherlands.(23) Pope Gregory XIII altered the Julian calendar, initiating a *new calendar* called the Gregorian, which eliminated 10 days by making October 5th to be October 15th. This was *464 years* after 1118 AD when a light appeared in the sky more brilliant that the sun, followed by a great cold spell, famine and plague in Europe.(24) Counting *464 years* after 1582 is 2046.

> *Isometric Projection Interpretation*: In 2046
> a strange light will be seen in the sky and it
> will cause ruin and death in Europe, its ap-
> pearance *altering the calendar* (causing Earth
> to move, change its orbital position).

In 1556 the writings of Nostradamus were all over Europe. In January a quake killed 830,000 Chinese, as already mentioned, and this was followed two months later by a comet. This was *490 years* after 1066 when a comet-like object was seen just prior to the Norman invasion of England.(25) Geoffrey Gaimar's *Lestoire Des Englis* reports that the English people witnessed a fire in the sky that burned brilliantly, which came near to the earth, appeared to move erratically, then descended into the sea. In many places the forests caught fire.(26) William of Normandy conquered the last Saxon king, Harold. Counting *490 years* after 1556 is 2046.

> *Isometric Projection Interpretation*: Recall
> that Nostradamus enigmatically referred to
> the "proof of the Normans." This concerns a
> *sign*. Mass death will occur in China and the
> cataclysm will *end* the English dynasty when
> the *sign* (NIBIRU) appears in the sky.

In 1301 a comet appeared and was spectacular to behold.(27) This was a period referred to as the Seven Comets over Europe, from 1298-1314. This was *740 years* after 566 AD when brilliant lights in the sky appeared around the sun and the heavens looked to be on fire, as recorded by Gregory of Tours. (28) Counting *740 years* after 1301 is 2046.

> *Isometric Projection Interpretation*: In 2046
> people will look into the skies, day and night,
> and see fantastic and awe-inspiring phenom-
> ena.

In 1293 an earthquake killed 20,000 people at Kamakura, Japan. This was *753 years* after 540 AD when a total eclipse of the sun occurred according to the *Anglo-Saxon Chronicle*.(29) As sophisticated computers reveal that no eclipses occurred at the time (which are caused by the moon), this sun darkening episode had to have been caused by some unknown body transiting between earth and the sun, casting at least parts of the British Isles in shadow. Also in this year the bubonic plague began in Justinian's domains in the eastern Roman Empire, spreading to Europe. Counting *753 years* after 1293 is 2046.

> *Isometric Projection Interpretation*: In 2046
> seismic activity will afflict Japan and the Far
> East with a terrible toll on life, while over
> Europe the sun will be obscured. A global
> epidemic will reach the western world.

In 1202 at the height of the famine in Egypt, a series of quakes began that were felt as far away as Syria. The destruction was widespread and reviewed in the previous chapter. This was *844 years* after 358 AD when disastrous earthquakes shook the areas of Macedonia, Asia, Pontus, and the metropolis of Bithynia, which received the worst. At dawn on August 24th the sky quickly gave way to thick masses of dark clouds that descended to the ground, blotting out the sun, and casting the land into thick blackness.

Ammianus Marcellinus reported that the destruction *began from the sky* in the form of loud crashes, winds and fatal lightning blasts. Just as fast as it all appeared, the sky cleared again, the clouds vanished, the earthquakes stopped and the beautiful day reappeared – but was contrasted by the sickening visage of thousands of mangled and torn human bodies among the piles of debris and transfixed on splintered timbers. In this same year of 358, the Jewish rabbi Hillel III altered the natural Jewish calendar and replaced it with a *new fixed calendar*. Counting *844 years* after 1202 is 2046.

> *Isometric Projection Interpretation*: In 2046 amidst violent atmospheric storms and darkening of the skies, earthquakes will destroy cities and their inhabitants throughout the Black Sea to these nations bordering the Mediterranean Sea. Due to this disaster and others of the time, a new calendar will be adopted.

In 1117 AD a comet filled the sky, traveling towards the Orient from the *north*, and the moon turned blood red during an eclipse.(30) This was *929 years* after 188 AD when the Chinese (the Orient) recorded the appearance of a bright comet.(31) Counting *929 years* after 1117 AD is 2046.

> *Isometric Projection Interpretation*: In 2046 a celestial body traveling from the north will be clearly seen from the Far East and the moon will appear as the color of blood.

In 66 AD a comet appeared and was seen by those inhabiting the Roman Empire and Judea.(32) A plague devastated the city of Rome and outlying areas, the city filled with corpses.(33) The Jewish War began against the Romans occupying Palestine. The death toll of this war was catastrophic. This was *1980 years* after 1915 BC when planet NIBIRU appeared as a sky dragon over Mesopotamia causing earthquakes, plague fogs, lightning blasts and flooding – an event expounded upon in *Anunnaki Homeworld*. Incidentally, NIBIRU's total orbit is 792 years, and 66 Anno Domini (isometric epicentral year) was *792 months* into the Anno Domini calendar [66 years x 12 months is 792]. Counting *1980 years* after 66 AD is 2046.

> *Isometric Projection Interpretation*: In 2046
> NIBIRU will fill the sky and cause a world-
> wide series of disasters unlike anything that
> has been experienced by humankind in thou-
> sands of years.

There are literally hundreds of thousands of scientific theories. There are many millions of people who believe them. John Gordon made an astute observation when he declared that "Orthodox science works only because approximations are allowed."(34)   Hypotheses grow into neatly packaged theories that are passed off as facts because scientists leave for themselves plenty of room for error. Knowledge becomes indefinite because approximations allow for the manipulation of data in myriads of ways. The scientist is rarely proven wrong in his assertions because he often asserts nothing absolute at all. When juggling amorphous variables, the scientist assumes a body of knowledge that in essence maintains no exact, definite dimensions.

But what you have been presented within three short books is a *fixed* timeline of events, a matrix of interwoven histories that all resurface through space and time in 2040 and 2046. This is possible because they are orbital, and thus astronomical, chronologies. There are no approximations provided. This book does not set out to prove the existence of the orbital periods of planets Phoenix and NIBIRU. This was already provided in *When the Sun Darkens* (Phoenix) and *Anunnaki Homeworld* (NIBIRU). The book you are holding now is a supplement, merely adding to the knowledge already set in stone and published in the prior books. Because of the absence of approximates, knowledge is not taken away or lost. It can only be added to. Unfortunately, it is for these reasons that scientists today will be the greatest enemies to this work.

As the attorney employs Latin and obscures terminology when addressing the bench to conceal his art from the layman, as the mystic employs strange symbols and ambiguity to control the outcome of her doings, as the old prophets spoke in the language of universals to mask the particulars they sought to address, so too do the modern scientists base their predictions on approximations. It is safe for them. One cannot be pushed off of a foundation that he is not standing on.

Calendrical isometrics is a science and it can reveal many things to the sincere student. A unique discovery can be shown to be authentic, a hoax can be exposed (no matter how many believe it), a people of unknown pedigree today can be linked back to their ancestors, wars can be predicted, and with whom and, as we have seen, disasters can be foreseen – to the exact year. By recognizing this, we more clearly understand the Russian physicist Ouspensky:

> What is necessary first to understand is not
> that the future is formed by any separate acts
> of the present, but that the whole of the future
> is in unbroken continuity with the present, as
> the present is with the past.(35)

As we found, Mother Shipton's life was intrinsically connected with the object of her message. She was born in the same year that planet Phoenix silently passed through the inner system in 1488. So too do we find an interesting parallel concerning the year Nostradamus was born.

In 1503 a windstorm dislodged a huge chunk of rock from a high mountain overlooking the sea at Naples, Italy. Inside the rock, a gathering of people discovered the huge fossil of a wooden ship with a design unlike any of them were familiar with. An Italian historian and statesman named Gionvanni Pontano was one of these witnesses who studied the amazing find.(36) This was the year Nostradamus was born.

When Nostradamus was 37 years old in 1540, Spanish miners searching for silver and gold traces near Calloa, Peru removed earth in a deep mineshaft and were astounded to find an entombed wooden vessel of extreme antiquity of an unconventional design.(37) Shortly afterward, back on the other side of the Atlantic, in Berne, Switzerland, miners digging for metals in the nearby mountains at a depth of 100 feet came upon the remains of an underground ship carved with well-fashioned ornamentation. Its masts were broken and an iron anchor was found. But to the horror of the miners they also discovered among the timbers the skeletons of forty men.(38)

In order to comprehend the relevance of these archeological discoveries one would have to know the history of planet Phoenix. Phoenix was named by Nostradamus and dated to return in 2040, which would be his message as recorded in the *Centuries*, which were composed during his life. These discoveries, made during his life, starting with the year of his birth, are relative because these landmasses that covered these three entombed ships were formed in 2239 BC during the one-year long global cataclysm known as the Great Flood. In this year, planet Phoenix darkened the sun after remaining visible for seven days and initiated the Deluge. These three ships were buried ever since that tragic catastrophe. They were unearthed during the life of the prophet who, over 37 centuries later, would record Phoenix's *return*.

Summary

The present is both a necessary consequence
of the past and the cause of the future.
                    —*C. W. Dalton, 1985* (1)

Though we began this study by employing the analogy of the pool of water and its ripples, we conclude with yet a more penetrating symbol for the phenomenon of time. The pendulum with regularity swings back and forth, keeping a natural rhythm. As it traverses its path of motion the pendulum spends the *majority* of its movement to the left or to the right of its 90° epicenter, moving into swings backward and forward before passing at its *quickest speed* over the epicenter that it crossed over in a blink.

Translated into the phenomenon of time, we find that the pendulum [material reality] spends an equal amount of its time to the left [the past] and to the right [the future], while spending hardly *no time at all* over the epicenter [the present], which it passes over rapidly as it moves *forward and backward* through space. By recognizing that we move *through* conditions that we perceive as events through our senses, we are better able to understand and study the world we live in, where it has been and where it is going. As *we* are the pendulums, the present barely exists at all, while the future continually flows into the past. As products of our own psyche, which is grounded in experience, it can be argued that the past and the future are more substantive than the present – the present being more illusory than that which was and which will be. Immanuel Kant in *Critique of Pure Reason* summed it up nicely when he wrote, "It is not time that passes, but the existence of what is changeable passes in time."(2)

93

The operation of the human mind reflects this phenomenon. Every day we find ourselves wrapped up in memories of the past or we worry about the future. Few people realize what is happening to them. When the human body is active, focused on something and concentrating, the present becomes more real to them. But when we stop moving, stop studying or meditating on a task, *immediately* the mind travels into the past or, by the agency of imagination, traverses the future, be it through hope or worry. When we are still, often without realizing it, our mind takes us backward and forward in time.

Over sixteen centuries ago Augustine of Hippo in *Confessions*, Book XI, pondered these things and was remarkably correct in his assessment. He wrote, "Time flies so quickly from future into past that it is an interval without duration. If it has duration, it is divisible into past and future. But the present occupies no space."(3) It is this author's own proposal that if we are able to perceive the existence of a phenomenon, then there must also be a method by which we can understand its basic mechanics. This led to my discovery (or maybe re-discovery, after Nostradamus) of timeline-based isometric projections.

The pendulum is our compass; the center of the device serves as our isometric epicenter. For the purposes of example, our center is 1973. If the distance the pendulum traveled was segmented into units we call years, then whatever year the swing of the pendulum attained going in one direction, it would again reach when traveling in the *opposite* direction. As with most of the laws of nature, the phenomenon is simple.

For Nostradamus to have seen the future and dated the events would have required him to have an accurate knowledge of the past, chronologies that would have covered a mere 500 to 550 years. He could have easily measured out multitudes of timelines that would have revealed to him the years 2040 and 2046. As any Nostradamus scholar is aware, Nostradamus *destroyed* his notes and his source materials. This he admitted.

The French seer had a method available to him but this does not exclude any other methods of predicting future events unknown to this author. That Mother Shipton also divined these events infers that revelation came in some other way. But human receptivity to perceived phenomena is not always expressed in the same ways. Two different people could come to the same conclusions, both being correct, though both interpreted what they perceived very differently from one another. That the Northern Prophetess and the French prophet lived at the same time hints at a greater link between those things that they had independently perceived.

This author claims no divine revelation or mystical guidance in coming to his conclusions about the global destructions of 2040 and 2046. His own research resulted from perceiving mathematical patterns between scores of similar events over periods of thousands of years that, when scrutinized carefully, reveal two different orbital chronologies of two planetary bodies that do not orbit the sun on the plane of the ecliptic as the other planets do, but both maintain orbits at extreme inclinations that are highly elliptical.

As stated previously, this book does not set out to prove the existence of these two planets, Phoenix and NIBIRU, but is a supplement to that earlier research. The reader is encouraged to read those other books and determine for himself that point in time when the many "coincidences" give way to no coincidence at all.

J. M. Breshears, 2012

Appendix

In *When the Sun Darkens* we are provided with a *fixed* chronology of orbital passes through the inner solar system of planet Phoenix every 138 years. This astronomical timeline of 138-year orbits is unbroken to 2040 AD.

In *Anunnaki Homeworld* we are provided with the orbital chronology of planet NIBIRU, a *fixed* 792-year orbit to 2046 AD. NIBIRU's orbit is eccentric and unusually elliptical, more like a comet, traveling for 732 years outside of the solar system through the Kuiper Belt, but spending 60 years at its visitation as it orbits the sun.

These two planets mark the beginning and the end of world *chronology*, a vast timeline understood by our predecessors. This chronology, entirely orbital, is now provided. The ONLY dates listed are those when Phoenix and NIBIRU appeared. The entries now contain the newer Phoenix and NIBIRU discoveries not known when this author's prior books on these subjects were published.

Fixed Chronology of the World

4309 BC   Phoenix appears in inner solar system during interplanetary cataclysm that leaves Earth in ruins as depicted in *Enuma Elish* of Babylon and Egyptian Gnostic texts *Trimorphic Protennoia* and *On the Origin of the World*. Phoenix is *named* in the Gnostic texts. A dust cloud hides the sun at this time according to Sumerian *Holy Tablets* and Earth is frozen. This was the destruction of the Pre-Adamic World hinted at in biblical passages.

4171 BC   Phoenix passes (138 yrs.)

4033 BC   Phoenix passes (138 yrs.)

3895 BC   Phoenix passes on 138 yr. orbit appearing as a "fiery flaming sword." Many historical texts describe celestial objects as flaming swords in the skies. In this year Mankind begins a prophesied 6000 years of banishment that will end in 2106 AD. This began the original Hebrew calendar until rabbinical corruption.

3757 BC   Phoenix passes (138 yrs.)

3619 BC   Phoenix passes (138 yrs.)

3499 BC   NIBIRU enters solar system beginning 60 years around the sun before exiting. In *The Holy Tablets* we find that the ancient Sumerians *knew* that NIBIRU passes 60 years after it appears.

3481 BC   Phoenix passes (138 yrs.)

3439 BC   NIBIRU passes close to earth as it exits solar system, completing 792-year orbit; global disaster kills a *third* of humanity according to Hebraic *Book of Jasher*, Haggadah texts. Babylonian tablets read that some of the Anunnaki descended to earth at this destruction and this is retold in the *Book of Enoch*. This is the *First Visitation* of Mother Shipton's sky-dragon.

3343 BC   Phoenix passes (138 yrs.)

3205 BC   Phoenix passes (138 yrs.) This is the 3rd year of Enoch's reign before the Flood. Many ancient traditions link Enoch with the legends of the Phoenix.

3067 BC   Phoenix passes (138 years)

2929 BC   Phoenix passes (138 years). Before Phoenix returns in 138 years the entire Great Pyramid/Giza complex would be constructed, requiring 90 years of building and quarrying.

2791 BC   Phoenix passes (138 yrs.) 24 years after the completion of the Great Pyramid. Noah was 48 years old.

2707 BC   NIBIRU enters solar system beginning 60 years around the sun. No records.

2653 BC   Phoenix passes (138 yrs.)

2647 BC   NIBIRU exits solar system completing 792-year orbit. No records.

2515 BC   Phoenix passes (138 yrs.) 300 years after completion of the Great Pyramid.

2377 BC   Phoenix passes (138 yrs.)

2239 BC   Phoenix passes in direct transit after being seen by the people of Earth for seven days, approaching like a fiery sword. The sun darkens, quakes shake the world, a large meteorite or comet slams into North America and another into Central America, and the Great Flood lays the world waste for an entire year. Too many historical references to be mentioned here.

2101 BC   Phoenix passes (138 yrs.)

1963 BC   Phoenix passes (138 yrs.)

1915 BC   NIBIRU enters solar system beginning 60 year pass around the sun. The ancients referred to it as a celestial dragon, or sky dragon, calling it Tiamat in Babylonia or Typhon in Egypt and the Aegean. It was a fiery red dragon that brought ruin to the earth, as also recorded in Hesiod's *Theogany*. This is Mother Shipton's *Second Visitation* of the sky dragon.

1855 BC   NIBIRU exits solar system, completing 792-year orbit. No records.

1825 BC   Phoenix passes (138 yrs.). This is the final year of Abraham's ministry in Egypt at the Great Pyramid complex and city of Annu, translating the antediluvian (pre-flood) records that were discovered there. This is the subject of this author's *Lost Scriptures of Giza*.

1687 BC   Phoenix passes (138 yrs.) in direct transit, darkening the sun and causing global earthquakes and floods that fell many of the ancient Old Bronze Age megalithic cities. This is *552 years* after the Flood. Disaster mentioned in the *Book of Jasher*, dated exactly by biblical chronologist Stephen Jones in *Secrets of Time*, described perfectly by W. J. Perry in *Children of the Sun*, by Augustine and Marcus Varro. In this year it was seen and called NINSIANNA by the Hittites.

1549 BC   Phoenix passes (138 yrs.)

1411 BC   Phoenix passes (138 yrs.). Israelites under Moses defeat the Amorites and kings, both giants named Sihon and Og of Bashan, descendants of the Anunnaki. Phoenix unseen.

1273 BC   Phoenix passes (138 yrs.). In this year Assyria becomes an empire, annexing Babylon and adopting the Winged Disk [Phoenix] as their official seal. Obscuration of the sun recorded in annals of Hittite King Mursilis II.

1135 BC   Phoenix passes (138 yrs.) in direct transit, darkening the sun. It is recorded by Nebuchadnezzar I of Babylon and by the Egyptians at the death of King Sethnakht, who wrote that the sun turned blood red and that *dust* blanketed the land. The sun darkened at this time during the war between the Tuatha de Danaan and the giants in ancient Ireland. Atreus of the Argives, an astronomer, predicts the darkening of the sun accurately and is chosen to lead his people. This was *552 years* after the 1687 Old Bronze Age cataclysm.

1123 BC   NIBIRU enters solar system beginning 60 years around the sun. The broken planet cast a shadow over the Far East and China was plagued by disasters ending the Shang Dynasty. About 250,000 Chinese took to the Pacific and vanished into the Americas. This was the *Third Visitation* of the sky dragon mentioned by Mother Shipton.

1063 BC   NIBIRU exits solar system after 60 years around the sun, completing 792 year orbit. No record.

997 BC   Phoenix passes (138 yrs.) and there is much evidence from the Old Testament that David recorded the appearance of Phoenix in the Psalms. He was 42 years old. Scientists estimate that at this time a meteorite struck North America in the Montana region.

859 BC   Phoenix passes (138 yrs.). First regnal year of Shalmaneser III of Assyria. At this year Elijah the prophet challenged the prophets of Baal. Fire from heaven descended and burnt the prophet's sacrifice, which was followed days later by an earthquake. The Phoenix is depicted on the famous Black Obelisk of Shalmaneser III.

721 BC   Phoenix passes (138 yrs.) Augustine, relying on Varro, relates that a strange darkening of the sun occurred but that it was not the moon. This corresponds to a major biblical event. Assyrian king, Shalmaneser V, sieged the Israelite city of Samaria in 723 BC. Sargon II of Assyria destroyed Samaria and enslaved the Israelites, deporting them to the northern and eastern frontiers of Assyria.

583 BC   Phoenix passes (138 yrs.) in direct transit, darkening the sun during a battle between the Lydians and Medes as recorded by Herodotus. This was *552 years* after 1135 BC when Nebuchadnezzar I ruled and recorded the appearance of Phoenix. Amazingly, in 583 BC *Nebuchadnezzar II* was ruling over Babylon. Thales of Miletus became famous for predicting the exact year the sun would darken (583 BC). Japanese regnal lists begin in this year.

445 BC   Phoenix passes (138 yrs.)

331 BC   NIBIRU enters solar system, beginning 60 years around the sun. There are no records of its appearance, but in this most famous year in history Alexander of Macedon defeats the Persian army in the Battle of Gaugamela, becoming Alexander the Great. He becomes king of Greece, Egypt, Persia and Babylon.

307 BC   Phoenix passes (138 years). No records, but this is the same year that Asoka of India sends out 80,000 Buddhist missionaries all over the east, Middle east and Mediterranean.

271 BC   NIBIRU exits solar system after 60 years around the sun, completing its 792 year orbit. No records.

169 BC   Phoenix passes (138 yrs.)

31 BC   Phoenix passes (138 yrs.). During the Battle of Actium between Octavian and Marcus Antony's forces (who were allied with Cleopatra of Egypt), a devastating earthquake afflicted Greece and Judea. Phoenix did not transit, falling out of alignment with earth. This was *552 years* after 583 BC. 31 BC is the final year engraved upon an Olmec date stele in Central America.

108 AD   Phoenix passes (138 yrs.).

246 AD   Phoenix passes (138 yrs.).

384 AD   Phoenix passes (138 yrs.).

462 AD   NIBIRU enters solar system, beginning 60 years around the sun. No records.

522 AD   NIBIRU exits solar system, passing closer to earth while completing its 792-year orbit. Planet Phoenix also enters inner system and passes Earth, this being the *only* year in world history that two intruder planets enter the inner system in the same year. In this year a series of destructive earthquakes afflict Olympia and Greece. This is the *Fourth Visitation* of Mother Shipton's sky dragon.

660 AD   Phoenix passes (138 yrs.). Dark Ages, no records.

798 AD   Phoenix passes (138 yrs.). Dark Ages.

936 AD   Phoenix passes (138 yrs.). Dark Ages.

1074 AD   Phoenix passes (138 yrs.). Dark Ages.

1212 AD   Phoenix passes (138 yrs.). Middle Ages.

1254 AD   NIBIRU enters solar system, beginning 60 years around the sun. Middle Ages, no records.

1314 AD   NIBIRU exists solar system after 60 years around the sun, completing 792-year orbit. Sun darkens over China, earthquakes and lightning storms attended with plague fogs and flooding. Over Europe the night sky is filled with a great blackness that blocks out the stars. This ends the period known as the Seven Comets over Europe. Meteorites crash into the Far East. *Fifth Visitation* of Mother Shipton's sky dragon.

1350 AD   Phoenix passes (138 yrs.).

1488 AD   Phoenix passes (138 yrs.). Ursula Southeil, or Mother Shipton, is born.

1626 AD   Phoenix passes (138 yrs.). New Amsterdam founded, later to be renamed New York. When Mother Shipton died in 1561, another famous person was born. . . Sir Francis Bacon. Intriguingly, in this year of 1626 Sir Francis Bacon now dies. Between the Phoenix visitations of 1488 and 1626 Mother Shipton was born, died, then Sir Francis Bacon is immediately born and then dies, with both life spans falling within the 138 years.

1764 AD   Phoenix passes (138 yrs.) and is seen by many thousands of people in Europe with the naked eye as it darkened one-fifth of the sun's surface. It was also observed by the astronomer Hoffman through a telescope.

1902 AD   Phoenix passes (138 yrs.) and blankets the earth in thousands of tons of cosmic dust, some of it falling to earth as mud. Phoenix brought with it comet Morehouse. New York City boasts the world's first skyscraper, the Fuller Building. The Babylonian *Enuma Elish* is translated into English (concerns 4309 Phoenix cataclysm) and the *Book of Enoch* is also published in English. 1902 is specifically encoded in Nostradamus' writings.

2040 AD   Phoenix passes (138 yrs.) in direct transit, darkening the sun and causing a pole shift. The earth's lithosphere slips over the mantle as entire continents are moved from their places. Quakes, volcanoes, tidal waves and electromagnetic storms are accompanied with meteoritic rain and a dense blanket of dust falling from the skies, as the moon turns a dull red. The Sixth Seal of the Apocalypse, a *fourth* of mankind dies. This is dated by Nostradamus, as discovered by Mario Reading. Coupled with 2046, this is the *SIXTH Visitation* of the sky dragon, prophesied by Mother Shipton, the prophetess who believed that both global catastrophes will be caused by the same (6th) sky dragon.

2046 AD   NIBIRU enters the solar system beginning 60 years around the sun. As it enters it passes dangerously close to Earth and initiates a second interplanetary catastrophe as quakes, volcanoes, electromagnetic storms, meteoric fallout and oceanic chaos kill a *third* of humanity that had survived the 2040 disasters six years earlier. This is the Trumpet judgments of Revelation. Dated by Nostradamus, as discovered by Mario Reading.

2106 AD   NIBIRU exits solar system after 60 years around the sun, completing its 792-year orbit. It is absolutely incredible that this is also the year 6000 from 3895 BC – when mankind was originally banished from paradise and when Phoenix appeared as a fiery flaming sword (symbol for judgment). The year 6000 brings *Armageddon*. As 3895 BC was not the beginning of humanity, merely the start of a timeline counting down to redemption, nor does the 6000 years indicate an end to man. It is a *beginning*. As found in *When the Sun Darkens*, the 6000 year timeline was dated and discovered by Stephen Jones and published in *Secrets of Time* – a man having no knowledge of planets Phoenix or NIBIRU, but who dated the events of the Bible by cross-referencing them with historical sources and the Assyrian Eponyms.

Calendrical isometrics works because the synthesis of these two distinct orbital chronologies remain *fixed* over thousands of years because these timelines are *astronomical*. Planet Phoenix *began* a countdown to apocalypse but planet NIBIRU *ends* this pattern. The reader need realize that this chronology is by no means complete. Everything you have read was put together in a Texas prison cell. There will no doubt be many others who will come forth with findings and discoveries further validating this thesis that the author was unaware of.

In 1781 Immanuel Kant, in his *Critique of Pure Reason*, wrote ". . .the appearances of past time determine every existence in succeeding time; and that these existences, as events, cannot take place except insofar as the appearance of past time determine their existence in time, that is, *fix it by a rule*."

This work is but an attempt.

Bibliography

Nostradamus 2: Into the Twenty-First Century: Jean-Charles de Fontbrune, trans. Alexis Lykiard (Henry Holt)

The Mask of Nostradamus: James Randi, 1990 (Charles Scribner's Sons)

Nostradamus: A Life and Myth: John Hogue, 2003 (Element)

Nostradamus and the Millennium: John Hogue, 1987 (A Dolphin Book)

The Final Prophecies of Nostradamus: Erika Cheetham, 1989 (Perigee Books)

Nostradamus: The Complete Prophecies for the Future: Mario Reading, 2006 (Watkins Publishing, London)

Nostradamus: The Lost Manuscript: Ottavio Cesare Ramotti, 1998 (Destiny)

The Secrets of Nostradamus: David Ovason (Harper Collins)

Tertium Organum: P.D. Ouspensky, 1919 (reprint Book Tree)

Secrets of Time: Stephen Jones (Gods Kingdom Ministries)

Technics and Civilization: Lewis Mumford (Harcourt Brace & World, Inc.)

Hyperspace: Michio Kaku, 1994 (Anchor Books, Oxford)

Gerald Massey's Lectures: Gerald Massey, 1900 (reprint Book Tree)

Three Books of Occult Philosophy: Henry Cornelius Agrippa, 16th cent. annot. by Donald Tyson (Llewellyn)

Critique of Pure Reason: Immanuel Kant, 1781, trans. Max Muller (Penguin)

The Portable Voltaire: edited by Ben Ray Redman, 1968 (Penguin)

The Story of Philosophy: Will Durant, 1926 (2006 Pocket Books)

The Discourses: Nicolo Machiavelli (Penguin)

Descartes: Key Philosophical Writings: trans. Elizabeth S. Haldane & G.R.T. Ross, 1997 (Wordsworth Classics)

The Myth of Sisyphus: Albert Camus 1942, trans. from French Justin O'Brien (Vintage)

Civilization or Barbarism?: Cheikh Anta Diop (Lawrence Hill Books)

The World As I See It: Albert Einstein, 1935 (reprint Book Tree)

The World's All Wrong: Everybody Knows It, But Nobody Wants to Admit It: C. W. Dalton, 1985 (A Big Blue Book)

The Decline of the West: Oswald Spengler: abridged edition by Helmut Werner, 1991)

Breaking the Godspell: The Politics of Our Evolution: Neil Freer, 2000 (Book Tree)

The Hidden Power: And Other Papers on Mental Science: Thomas Troward, 1921 (reprint Book Tree)

The Synagogue of Satan: Andrew Carrington Hitchcock (Rivercrest Pub.)

The Book of the Damned: Charles Fort, 1919 (Bonnie & Liveright, NY/reprint Book Tree)

The Gods of Eden: William Bramley (Avon)

Cataclysm! Compelling Evidence of a Cosmic Catastrophe in 9500 BC: D.S. Allen & J.B. Delair (Bear & Co.)

Ages in Chaos, Vols. I & II: Immanuel Velikovsky, 1978 (reprint 2010 Paradigma)

Great Disasters:(Readers Digest Assoc.) edited Kaari Ward, 1989

Natural Disasters: Readers Digest Assoc. 1996

The Science-Times Book of Natural Disasters: edited Nicholas Wade, 2000 (The Lyons Press)

Introduction to Comets: John C. Brandt & Robert D. Chapman, 2004 (Cambridge Univ. Press)

Apocalypse 2012: An Investigation into Civilization's End: Lawrence E. Joseph 2007 (Broadway Books)

Pole Shift: John White (ARE Press)

Lost Scriptures of Giza: Enochian Mysteries of the World's Oldest Texts: Jason M. Breshears, 2006 (Book Tree)

When the Sun Darkens: Orbital Chronology and 2040 AD Return of Planet Phoenix: Jason M. Breshears, 2009 (Book Tree)

Anunnaki Homeworld: Orbital Chronology and 2046 AD Return of Planet NIBIRU: Jason M. Breshears, 2011 (Book Tree)

The End of Eden: The Comet That Changed Civilization: Graham Phillips, 2007 (Bear & Co.)

Fingerprints of the Gods: Graham Hancock, 1995 (Mandarin)

Egypt: Child of Atlantis: John Gordon, 1997 (Bear & Co.)

Survivors of Atlantis: Frank Joseph, 2004 (Bear & Co.)

A Hitchhiker's Guide to Armageddon: David Hatcher Childress (Adventures Unlimited)

The End of Days: Armageddon and Prophecies of the Return: Zechariah Sitchin, 2006 (William Morrow)

Alexandria: Jewel of Egypt: Jean-Yves Emperrur, trans. Jane Brenton (Discoveries, Abrams, 2001)

Children of the Sun: A Study of the Egyptian Settlement of the Pacific: W. J. Perry, 1923 (reprint Adventures Unlimited)

Voyages of the Pyramid Builders: Robert Schoch & Robert McNally (Tarcher Putnam)

The Great Pyramids: Jean-Pierre Corteggiani (Discoveries, Abrams, NY)

Ancient Mysteries: Peter James & Nick Thorpe (Ballantine)

Secret Cities of Old South America: Harold T. Wilkins, 1952 (Adventures Unlimited)

The Naked Olympics: The True Story of the Ancient Games: Tony Perrottet 2004 (Random House trade)

1066 The Year of the Conquest: David Howarth (Barnes & Noble)

History in Quotations: Reflecting 5000 Years in World History: M.J. Cohen and John Major (Cassel)

The Golden Treasury of Patristic Quotations: From 50-750 AD, compiled by I.D.E. Thomas, 1996 (Hearthstone Press)

Alice in Wonderland and the World Trade Center Disaster: David Icke, 2002 (Bridge of Love)

Sargon the Magnificent: Mrs. Sidney Bristowe (The Assassination of the Covenant People)

In Search of Noah's Ark: David Balsiger & Charles E. Sellier, Jr. (Sun Classic Books)

The Nag Hammadi Library: Definitive Translation of the Gnostic Scriptures: James M. Robinson (Harper San Francisco)

The Annals of Imperial Rome: Tacitus, trans. Michael Grant (Penguin)

The Later Roman Empire: Ammianus Marcellinus: trans. Walter Hamilton (Penguin)

Enuma Elish: Seven Tablets of Creation: Vol. I & II, L.W. King, 1902 (Book Tree)

Saint Augustine: Confessions: trans. Henry Chadwick, 1992 (Oxford Univ. Press)

The City of God: Saint Augustine, trans. Marcus Dods, 2009 (Hendrickson Pub.)

The Secret in the Bible: Tony Bushby (Joshua Books)

Magic: White and Black: Franz Hartmann, M. D. 1888 (Book Tree reprint)

Crop Circles, Gods and Their Secrets: Robert Boerman (Frontier/Adventures Unlimited)

Of Heaven and Earth: edited Zecharia Sitchin (Book Tree)

Antigravity and the World Grid: David Hatcher Childress (Adventures Unlimited)

Our Haunted Planet: John Keel, 1971 (reprint Galde Press)

Invisible Residents: Ivan T. Sanderson, 1970 (Adventures Unlimited)

Atlantis: Kingdom of the Neanderthals: Colin Wilson, 2006 (Bear & Co.)

The Greek Myths: Robert Graves (Penguin)

The Complete Story of the San Francisco Horror: Hubert D. Russell, 1906 (2003 (reprint Book Tree)

Notes and Sources

I.   *Introduction to Calendrical Isometrics*

1.   The Myth of Sisyphus 12

2.   Oliver Wendell Holmes

3.   Antigravity and the World Grid 129

4.   The World As I See It 29

5.   Hyperspace 232

6.   Tertium Organum 43

7.   Tertium Organum 68

8.   The Golden Treasury of Patristic Sayings 91

9.   Crop Circles, Gods and Their Secrets 139

10.   The End of Days 311

11.   City of God Book 16

12.   Three Books of Occult Philosophy 673

13.   Discourses I: 38-39, 43-48 pgs. 207, 517

14.   Lectures 246, 277

15.   Magic 29

16.   The Decline of the West 46

17.   The Hidden Power 13

18.   Descartes 11

19.   Technics and Civilization 15

20.   The Decline of the West 73

21.   Augustine of Hippo 223

22.   Conscious Healing: Sol Luckman, The Janus Program, Beth Goobie, Paranoia magazine, Spring 2008, p. 9

II.   *Planet Phoenix: Keeper of the Calendar*

1. The Portable Voltaire 223
2. Enuma Elish lines 1-3 pg. 3
3. The Nag Hammadi Library 517-518
4. The Nag Hammadi Library 186-188
5. The Holy Tablets 76, pg. 5 col. 2
6. City of God: Augustine Book 15
7. Survivors of Atlantis 63
8. Survivors of Atlantis 60
9. City of God: Augustine Book 21
10. Survivors of Atlantis 66
11. Fingerprints of the Gods 383
12. Ages in Chaos Vol. I p. 65
13. Sargon the Magnificent 165, citing Prof. Waddell
14. History in Quotations 3
15. Survivors of Atlantis 31-32
16. Survivors of Atlantis 68
17. 1 Kings 18:38, 19:11-12
18. City of God; Augustine Book 3
19. Ages in Chaos Vol. II 142-144
20. Time-Encyclopedia Britannica 2008, p. 591 has it at 585 BC
21. Breaking the Godspell 41
22. The Naked Olympics 191
23. Nostradamus 2 p. 28
24. Nostradamus: The Lost Manuscript 79
25. The Secrets of Nostradamus 104
26. The Secrets of Nostradamus 118-119
27. Nostradamus: The Lost Manuscript 27

III.   *The Date-Index of Nostradamus*

1. Nostradamus' Letter to Henry, King of France

2. Nostradamus: A Life and Myth 157

3. The Decline of the West 52

4. Natural Disasters 14

5. The Mask of Nostradamus 18

6. Fingerprints of the Gods 512

7. Introduction to Comets 3

8. Pole Shift 256

9. Nostradamus: The Lost Manuscript 78-79

IV.   *The Sky-Dragons of 2040 and 2046 AD*

1. The Hidden Power 3

2. The Mask of Nostradamus 132

3. Of Heaven and Earth p. 141

4. The Story of Philosophy 134-135

5. The Mask of Nostradamus 132

6. Apocalypse 2012 p. 165

7. The Synagogue of Satan 25

8. The Story of Philosophy 198

9. The Synagogue of Satan 61

V.   *Isometric Projections of 2040 AD*

1. Ages in Chaos Vol. I, p. 337

2. Cataclysm! 353

3. The Science Times Book of Natural Disasters 188

4. Our Haunted Planet 178

5. Book of the Damned 51, 222

6. Book of the Damned 211

7. Book of the Damned 176

8. Introduction to Comets 16

9. Cataclysm! 200

10. Introduction to Comets 16

11. Book of the Damned 37

12. Great Disasters 176

13. Book of the Damned 138

14. Book of the Damned 207

15. Of Heaven and Earth, p. 142, Antonio Huneeus

16. Great Disasters 65

17. Great Disasters 55

18. History of the Later Roman Empire Bk. 26, p. 333

19. Book of the. Damned 166

20. The Rosicrucian Cosmo-Conception 513-514

21. Book of the Damned 155

22. The End of Eden 163

23. Hyperspace 294-295

24. The Rosicrucian Cosmo-Conception 513

25. Book of the Damned 177

26. Introduction to Comets 380-381

27. Gods of Eden: Bramley 184

28. Nostradamus: A Life and Myth XV-XVIII

29. Introduction to Comets 16

30. Alexandria 70

31. Gods of Eden: Bramley 149

32. Natural Disasters 50

33. Alice in Wonderland and the World Trade Center Disaster 128

34. The Hidden Power 26-27

VI.   *Isometric Projections of 2046 AD*

1. Children of the Sun 17

2. Cataclysm! 200

3. Book of the Damned 217

4. Cataclysm! 352

5. Book of the Damned 155

6. Cataclysm! 350

7. Secrets of Nostradamus 293

8. Civilization or Barbarism 69

9. In Search of Noah's Ark 58

10. Book of the Damned 211-212

11. Introduction to Comets 16

12. Cataclysm! 350

13. Book of the Damned 178

14. Of Heaven and Earth, p. 142, Antonio Huneeus

15. Introduction to Comets 16

16. Introduction to Comets 277

17. The Great Pyramid: Corteggiani 32

18. Natural Disasters 50

19. Introduction to Comets 6

20. The Secret in the Bible 123

21. Introduction to Comets 6

22. Introduction to Comets 13,16

23. Gods of Eden: Bramley 184

24. Gods of Eden: Bramley 183

25. 1066 The Year of the Conquest 83

26. Invisible Residents 32

27. Ancient Mysteries 160

28. Gods of Eden: Bramley 149

29. Voyages of the Pyramid Builders 214

30. Gods of Eden: Bramley 183, citing Noh1 at 56-57

31. Introduction to Comets 86

32. Ancient Mysteries 103

33. Tacitus; Annals XVI 10-13, p. 387

34. Child of Atlantis 5

35. Tertium Organum, citing Mabel Collins

36. Secret Cities of Old South America 417

37. Secret Cities of Old South America 418

38. Secret Cities of Old South America 417

Summary

1. The World's All Wrong 454

2. Critique of Pure Reason 180

3. Augustine of Hippo 232

About the Author

As of 2012 Jason M. Breshears has been in a south Texas prison for over 22 years, since he was 17 years old. He was given an agreed-to sentence that would require him to serve only seven and a half years. In 1999 he was granted his parole release but the Texas Parole Board adopted new retroactive policies that have since blocked his release. Though a model prisoner and published author, Jason has been denied parole release five times and been made to serve over twelve years more than what his original plea bargain with the State mandated. His situation is not an anomaly in the draconian system of Texas politics. Until he is released he continues his research and writing, and at 39 years of age has written the following works:

Lost Scriptures of Giza: Enochian Mysteries of the World's Oldest Texts. By gathering together knowledge from various holy books, ancient symbols and the oldest known writings of ancient Egypt, Breshears reveals patterns that can allow us to make future predictions. He advances the theory that all major cataclysms of the past occurred at specifically predicable times, and reveals when the next world-wide catastrophe will come. 1st ed. 256 pgs, 8.5 x 11, $29.95 (updated, 2nd ed. coming)

When the Sun Darkens: Orbital History and 2040 AD Return of Planet Phoenix. By using foundational scientific evidence and various prophecies, the return of the legendary Phoenix, an outer rogue planet that often brings destruction, is predicted. 128 pgs, 6 x 9, $14.95

Anunnaki Homeworld: Orbital History and 2046 AD Return of Planet Nibiru. The author uses scientific cycles, mathematical formulas, advanced geometry and historical records to predict the cataclysmic return of the most legendary rogue planet in the solar system. 164 pgs, 8.5 x 11, $19.95

Manuscripts completed and coming soon:
Descent of the Seven Kings: Anunnaki Chronology and 2052 AD Return of the Fallen Ones
Chronotecture: Lost Science of Prophetic Engineering
Chronicon: Timelines of the Ancient Future
King of the Giants: Mighty Hunter of World Mythology
The Book of Jason: Philosophical Musings of a Dark Prophet

TO ORDER CALL 1-800-700-TREE (8733) 24 hrs., all major cards accepted. Buy any two of the avail. titles, get 10% off and free shipping.

9 781585 091409